LONGING FOR AN ABSENT GOD

LONGING FOR AN ABSENT GOD
Faith and Doubt in Great American Fiction

Print ISBN: 978-1-5064-5195-4
eBook ISBN: 978-1-5064-5196-1

The names of the people included in this book have
been changed to protect their identities.

Cover design: Paul Soupiset

LONGING
FOR AN
ABSENT
GOD

**FAITH AND DOUBT IN
GREAT AMERICAN FICTION**

NICK RIPATRAZONE

fortress press

MINNEAPOLIS

For Amelia, Olivia, and Jennifer

CONTENTS

ACKNOWLEDGMENTS

Sections of this book previously appeared in different
forms in *Rolling Stone*, *The Atlantic*, *The Paris Review*,
The Sewanee Review, *Literary Hub*, *America*, and
Commonweal; I appreciate the support of those editors.

Heartfelt gratitude to my parents. Appreciation
to Dana Gioia for conversations about Catholic
literature in America. Many thanks to my editor,
Emily Brower, for her guidance and support of
this book, from idea to publication.

Olivia, Amelia, and Jennifer: all of this—
and everything else—is for you.

PREFACE

The story of a Catholic running for president in 1928 started in a church. Born of a poor family on the Lower East Side, Al Smith would rise to become the four-time governor of New York through personality and presence. Even the pugnacious critic H. L. Mencken couldn't help but praise Smith: "There is something singularly and refreshingly free, spacious, amiable, hearty, and decent about him."[1] Smith's years at St. James Roman Catholic Church taught him that faith was a powerful form of storytelling.

In the basement of that church, Smith honed his skills as a performer. "Dead stuck on acting," Smith appeared in amateur plays to much acclaim.[2] He became a gifted orator, "capable of dictating a speech from scratch, repeating it once or twice aloud, and having it memorized."[3] As an altar boy at St. James, Smith was surrounded by the mystery and grandeur of Mass, an experience that cemented his lifelong faith. Catholic storytelling, like

7

the Catholic Mass, is a mixture of performance and symbolism—and the confidence that derives from a liturgy that finds God in all things. Smith's grandson, later a Catholic priest, would say his grandfather "would die rather than miss Mass on Sunday."[4]

Smith paid a price for his piety. A northeastern Catholic whose campaign theme song was "The Sidewalks of New York"—with lyrics like "Boys and girls together, me and Mamie O'Rourke / Tripped the light fantastic on the sidewalks of New York"—Smith was lambasted as un-American and even un-Christian.[5] For segments of the Protestant electorate, he was by turns strange and dangerous; they worried his fidelity was to Rome, not Washington. Political cartoons portrayed the anti-Prohibition Smith as a bellboy, holding a jug of whiskey on a platter while he serves the pope and cardinals during a cabinet meeting. Breathless pamphlets warned that the Holland Tunnel would be a secret passageway between the Vatican and the White House.

Even the Ku Klux Klan got involved. They started with cartoons and mailings, but they had a surprise for him in Oklahoma: burning crosses. Smith battled back with a campaign speech in Oklahoma City, denouncing hate in the name of God. He ended his speech by saying that anyone who "votes against me because of my religion . . . is not a real, pure, genuine American."[6]

While Smith was traveling the country, fighting his uphill battle against anti-papist sentiment, his close friend was embarking on another type of journey. Father Fulton Sheen and Smith had dinner each Sunday night for years, and would travel to Europe together in 1937. Smith was convinced that Republican anti-Catholic rhetoric had originated with Herbert Hoover's campaign director, Horace Mann. Sheen began corresponding with Mann, who, along with his wife, later converted to Catholicism.

Sheen had a magical way with words, and the Word. Born in Illinois and ordained in 1919, he studied theology at the Catholic University of America, the Sorbonne, and the Collegio Angelico in Rome. His theological brilliance was matched by his penchant for performance. Father Sheen was a charismatic preacher. In 1928, the Paulist Fathers invited Father Sheen to give regular sermons during Lent before a live audience at the Church of St. Paul the Apostle in New York City, where radio towers rose to the sky next to the rectory.

Boasting one of the most powerful signals in the country, the Paulist-run WLWL was an evangelizing force, and it was where Sheen began honing a broadcasting style that would later be loved by many millions, Catholic and otherwise. "The vast church was filled upstairs and downstairs," Sheen would recall, with cushions and chairs provided "for the overflow crowd."[7] Reflecting on those years, Sheen once said, "Radio is like the Old Testament, for it is the hearing of the Word without the seeing."[8]

Sheen had the power of *story*, a power that would capture hearts and minds for years to come. During those same early months of 1928, another storyteller, the editor of *Columbia*—the magazine of the Knights of Columbus—was leaving his post. "I have decided that it is time to move," Myles Connolly wrote.[9] "A change of air will do me good."[10] A talented editor who regularly published luminaries such as G. K. Chesterton and Hilaire Belloc, Connolly was about to embark on his own literary adventure. His short novel *Mr. Blue* is a work of sincere, dogmatically faithful Catholic literature. A work, truly, from another era.

* * *

To conflate a quote from one Oscar Wilde play with the title of another, nowadays to be earnest is to be found out. Earnestness in secular literature has been gauche for years, but one of the greatest literary sins is frank depictions of religious belief. God forbid the writer who chooses conviction over irony. A character who authentically believes in God is strange, mad, or a liar. Sometimes all three.

How did this happen? Literary history is a story of responses and rejoinders, and the nineteenth-century ancestors of the modern Catholic novel were adherent to dogma. Today, the pendulum has swung in the complete opposite direction, where straightforward faith cannot be presumed. Religious art tends to be self-consciously devotional or distant. As the shadow of postmodernism extends to the present, Catholic writers are no longer ashamed of their rosaries. They often don't own any.

Consider the novels of self-described "agnostic Catholic" David Lodge.[11] In *The British Museum Is Falling Down*, Catholicism is the source of outmoded sexuality, a cultural millstone in the form of the rhythm method. Main characters Adam and Barbara Appleby already have three children and don't want another, but as practicing Catholics, they have little recourse. In a later novel, *Therapy*, Catholicism is a source of nostalgia, something Lodge's characters believed in before they grew up. The novel's usage of church symbolism, from the Virgin Mary to religious pilgrimage, remains firmly in the world of ironic symbol rather than credible belief.

The earnestly religious literary work is pious and unembarrassed about faith. The characters might struggle with belief; they might even lapse into doubt. Yet overall, earnest religious works exist as spiritual stories in a secular world, and not as stories in which belief is mere symbol. An earnest Catholic novel, in particular, would be dogmatically faithful. This is not to say that such a novel is more catechism than fiction, but instead that such a work stays true to Catholic faith in both content and method.

Such a description applies to Myles Connolly's novel. Mr. Blue is a mystic: part modern-day St. Francis, part itinerant monk. His eccentricity and unbridled joy might first confuse the contemporary reader, but the largely forgotten book is worth revisiting in the age of ironic religious fiction.

The novel is narrated and framed by an acquaintance of Blue, who is both fascinated and confounded by his saint-like subject. In a more contemporary work, this narrator would be dismissive of Blue, but in Connolly's vision, the narrator adopts a generous tone. What makes *Mr. Blue* fully earnest is that both the characters and the novelist are sincerely Catholic. An earnest character in the hands of an ironic writer would feel like parody. Mr. Blue, however ebullient, never becomes a joke.

Blue is whimsical. He has an affinity for trips and pilgrimages; the narrator calls him a "gallant monk without an order. Or perhaps his order was life and the world his monastery."[12] Mr. Blue ponders publishing a deluxe, decadently illustrated edition of the New Testament. He wants to make a film about a post-apocalyptic world where Christianity has been eliminated and where humans "were minor automatons, servants of a mechanical state."[13] He lives on top of a skyscraper, where he pantomimes Mass and wants the homeless of the city to join him: "Poor people with these horizons! Poor people with the whole beautiful world beneath them!"[14]

Blue is a millionaire through an inheritance. He buys estates, hires servants, and lets the servants have the homes. He entertains himself by spending his money as quickly as possible, and when he goes broke, he realizes "those millions were a trial set me by my Lady Poverty."[15] Cleansed of wealth, he embarks on a wild tour of grace, armed with the "boyishness of the true mystic."[16] The narrator might think Blue is insane, but divinely so.

Connolly, a screenwriter who was once nominated for an Oscar for *Music for Millions*, wrote more of an entertainment than a novel in *Mr. Blue*. It is not a work of intellectual latitude, but that is part of the book's appeal. The novel is written with the spirit of Mr. Blue, an odd, child-like man who "talked of life, the adventure of life, the loveliness of life."[17]

This is not to say that *Mr. Blue* is simplistic. Connolly was a deft writer. Early in the book, while the narrator is trying to understand his unusual friend, it is dusk in the street, and "students in a theological school nearby were practicing hymns. Lights were spurting out, street lights, window lights."[18] Connolly shows us Blue sleeping in an attic, where the scene is downright surreal:

> Behind the screen was a tall black cross mounted on a slight elevation. It was a brutal, bare cross. Before it, to one side, burned a candle. And on the floor, on his knees, his hands on the floor, his head almost on his hands, his hair barely out of reach of the smoky candle, knelt the erstwhile gay and gallant Blue. It was a striking picture, the black cross, the black figure, and the splotch of yellow candle.[19]

This is a pivot endemic to the Catholic literary mode: the swift ascent to the lyric, sensual, and hymnal.

The second half of *Mr. Blue* is slow, focused on Blue's letters to the narrator. The prose lacks the awe-induced immediacy of the early pages. Yet, there is still the occasional gem in the prose, as when Blue makes an impassioned call for a resurrection of authentic religious art in America. "The poet saw Christ on the Thames," he says.[20] "We might find him on the Hudson or the Charles."[21] He longs for "artists to immerse themselves in the fresh waters of the faith and come up vibrant, clean, alert to the world around them."[22] He is tired of religious writers speaking of the past: "Great men dominate their age with their own art. . . . They do not achieve greatness by fleeing the present or by bowing down in timid affection before the past. . . . No. They take contemporary life vividly into their arms and out of the union is born their art."[23] Sincere words, captured and curated by the narrator who concludes with Blue's wider statement that Catholic art is the best defense against "scientific agnosticism"; it offers another state of mind, another mode of being.[24]

While the narrator may not be as ardent a Catholic as Blue, he wishes he were, and that sense of respect permeates the book. Blue's strangeness arises from the same place as his genuineness. *Mr. Blue* is the story of a man who considers generosity and belief acts of cultural rebellion. It is a book of authentic, unbridled religious conviction. We might even call it a *sincerely* Catholic book.

Ninety years later, Catholic sincerity in literature, art, entertainment, and other forms of mainstream culture is muddled. The three top-rated late-night television show hosts—Stephen Colbert, Jimmy Fallon, and Jimmy Kimmel—are all Catholics. Colbert, a former Sunday school teacher whose nuanced understanding of theology nicely complements his irreverent humor, is perhaps the most popular and consistently sincere Catholic entertainer. The Catholic-educated Fallon, although now lapsed, grew up particularly attuned to the beauty and grandeur of Mass—so much so that he wanted to become a priest. Kimmel has spoken about his continued practice of Catholic faith with a vocal support for the priesthood that hearkens back to his days as an altar boy.

Oscar and Grammy award–winning singer Lady Gaga, born Stefani Joanne Angelina Germanotta, attended Sacred Heart School, a Catholic school in New York City. Catholic iconography and symbolism saturates her work, and she has not shied from speaking about her Catholic faith, past and present. Catholicism-as-spectacle was seen at the Metropolitan Museum of Art's 2018 showcase, "Heavenly Bodies: Fashion and the Catholic

Imagination"—their most-ever visited exhibit. Five of the nine Supreme Court justices are Catholic, and another was Catholic-raised and schooled, but attends an Episcopal church.

Catholicism is by no means rare in contemporary mainstream American culture, and the papacy of Pope Francis has brought a groundswell of secular attention, and often admiration, to Catholicism. Yet, contemporary Catholic practice and cultural representation is fragmented, with the lines between sincerity and parody often blurred.

Al Smith, Fulton Sheen, and Myles Connolly: three American Catholics whose sense of story was inextricable from their religious identity. Each man was publicly, sincerely *Catholic*. Their lives suggest a starting point for an examination of Catholic storytelling in *Longing for an Absent God*—a work that attempts to understand what has happened to God and fiction in the past ninety years.

INTRODUCTION

Does Belief Matter in Fiction?

The Iowa Writers' Workshop is a long way from Milledgeville, Georgia, but Flannery O'Connor felt at home during daily Mass at St. Mary's Catholic Church on East Jefferson Street in Iowa City. She was completing a thesis of stories and drafting *Wise Blood*, a novel that would contribute to her unique position as a deeply religious writer who is studied in secular classrooms across America. O'Connor's piety has never been a secret, but the recent publication of her prayer journal reveals the strength of her private exhortations: "Dear Lord, please make me want You. It would be the greatest bliss. Not just to want You when I think about You but to want You all the time, to think about You all the time, to have the want driving in me, to have it like a cancer in me. It would kill me like a cancer and that would be the Fulfillment."[1]

O'Connor said her kin were "given to such phrases as, 'Let's face it.'"[2] Let us face it. There will never be another Flannery

O'Connor; not in deed and certainly not in word. Her literary works included only two novels and two collections of short stories, but that small oeuvre has achieved canonical status. When the Library of America released her collected works in 1988, she was the first writer of her generation in the catalog, and the only woman from her century. Roughly a hundred book-length studies of her work have appeared as well as over a thousand articles, chapters, and essays. She earned a posthumous National Book Award for her collection, *The Complete Stories*, which was later voted the best work of fiction ever to receive the award.

She supplemented her fiction with a sharp critical sense formed by her Catholic identity. She added nuance to the connection between dogma and literature. Rather than a hindrance for writers, dogma was for her a means of freedom. Dogma is "not a set of rules which fixes [what the writer] sees in the world. It affects his writing primarily by guaranteeing his respect for mystery."[3] In her redefinition of the term, dogma recedes rather than prescribes; it creates an atmosphere and background for a work.

O'Connor loathed devotional fiction; work plied for the arrow of evangelization. Even a story like "Parker's Back," which concludes with a clever distinction between idolatry and iconography, ends with a scene of violence and regret. Her sermons were messy.

In "The Church and the Fiction Writer," O'Connor rails against weak fiction that only exists in deference to doctrinaire principles. These "sorry productions" are not the fault of the Church, but "of restrictions that [the writer] has failed to impose on himself."[4] The Church is a vessel of belief, not an instrument of art. To expect the mode of the latter in the world of the former is unrealistic. O'Connor believed the mysteries of faith demanded similarly mysterious tools in order to be made visible.

The Catholic writer, then, must pay homage to the work. "Your first concern," intones O'Connor, "will be the necessities that present themselves in the work."[5] Dogma is rigid; theology—the story—bends. Although O'Connor was profoundly Catholic, even in her private letters, she was far more concerned with a world-view than doctrine. "The good novelist not only finds a symbol for feeling," she writes, "he finds a symbol and a way of lodging it which tells the intelligent reader whether this feeling is adequate or inadequate, whether it is moral or immoral, whether it is good or evil. And his theology, even in its most remote reaches, will have a direct bearing on this."[6]

O'Connor thought that her passionate belief would not be shared by the majority of her readers, southern or otherwise: "you have to make your vision apparent by shock—to the hard of hearing you shout, and for the almost blind you draw large and startling figures."[7] She thought "distortion" was a necessary instrument. O'Connor did not shout to convert readers or to "prove the existence of the supernatural."[8] Those "low motives" become obvious when a story's "pertinent actions have been fraudulently manipulated or overlooked or smothered."[9] She held fiction to a higher standard. She was truly catholic in her reach and knew full well that she could not expect her readers to come to her pages valuing a rite such as baptism. She has to do the work, "to bend the whole novel—its language, its structure, its action."[10]

That standard either makes O'Connor a template for the writer of faith, or as Paul Elie has surmised, "our oppressor, whose genius makes clear what we lack."[11] Now, more than fifty years after O'Connor's death, what has become of the literature of Catholic faith? Are American Catholic writers as relevant to the wider literary and cultural conversation as O'Connor was in her lifetime? Are they published in the major mainstream literary magazines? Do they receive prestigious secular awards and fellowships? Or are they instead considered marginal, irrelevant, and antiquated because of their beliefs? Do contemporary writers of Catholic faith produce works that even merit serious literary consideration?

Dana Gioia has lamented that despite having more than seventy million members, Roman Catholicism "currently enjoys almost no positive presence in the American fine arts."[12] Gioia's bold claim describes a recent phenomenon and is particularly striking when we consider the previously "active role [Catholic voices] played in shaping the dynamic public conversation that is American literature."[13]

While Gioia recognizes the significant contributions of "dissident" Catholics, he is most interested in the stark contrast between "practicing Catholics [who] remain active in the Church" but are "currently the least visible in a literary culture," and the more notable contributions of cultural, or what I call lapsed, Catholics.[14] Gioia defines those Catholic writers as "raised in the faith and often educated in Catholic schools. Cultural Catholics usually made no dramatic exit from the Church but instead gradually drifted away. Their worldview remains essentially Catholic, though their religious beliefs, if they still have any, are often unorthodox."[15] These lapsed Catholics no longer practice; yet, they share a tangible Catholic formation through family, schooling, and early church attendance. Their writing not only reveals a Catholic milieu, but also a cultural one devoid of any transcendent faith. Catholicism may or may not be a subject in their work, but its influence is present. A discerning reader will notice the vestiges of their former belief.

Catholic belief and Catholic culture overlap, but they can also diverge. Lapsed Catholics—those raised in the religion but who have drifted from the practice—often retain emotional attachment to signifiers of that past faith. We are all drawn to the nostalgia of youth, but Catholics raised on a religion of mystery, image, smell, and song are particularly vulnerable to the pull of sentimentality. There is a feeling and language for this: Catholics call it to "go home."

Catholicism is an assault on the senses. The thickly sweet smell of incense clouding a church. A finger dipped into the holy water fount; the almost otherworldly touch of it. The feel of a back against the hard pew, or knees pushing through paltry cushions. The rise and refrain of hymns, belted in choral bursts, complemented by the silence of prayer. The Stations of the Cross lining the walls of the church: an itinerant narrative, casted and performed in the high drama of Lent, but a constant reminder of the most powerful Christian story. The crucifix itself: Christ's body raised from the wood—contorted, breathing, struggling.

At the front of the church is the priest: a celebrant, a mentor, a counselor. For older Catholics, the memory of Mass in Latin: theatrical, grand, solemn. That Mass was slowed down, life made surreal. Contemporary Mass, now celebrated in the local tongue, still retains that beautiful oddity of poetic language pushing toward the rafters. Catholicism is a communal faith.

Candles flicker at the feet of the Virgin Mary. Devotion to her extends outside the church. Front-lawn statues. Prayer cards. Candles bought at church basement-shops and supermarkets. The miraculous medal necklace which reads: "Mary conceived without sin, pray for us who have recourse to thee." The rosary as a daily devotion: a tactile tool, a litany, a narrative with discrete parts. It is a practice with its own folkloric texture—the belief that angels finish the prayers of those who fall asleep during the rosary. An equal devotion to the lives of the saints: lives of miracle and martyrdom. Saints were often, at some point, sinners: they showed the possibility of radical change. Saints intercede.

For some Catholics, these practices are daily, habitual. For others, they are occasional. For most, they are acutely understood in the same way we know our own families. Thomas Aquinas captured it best: Catholics believe in a God among us. God is not abstraction or artifact: God is present, and God is presence. In what priest and theologian David Tracy calls the analogical language of Catholicism, the body and blood of Christ at Mass are both symbol and reality.

Lapsed Catholics—those who have inspired the title of this book, *Longing for an Absent God*—feel the world is no longer tethered to this presence of God. As Catholics, they feel this loss most acutely. This does not mean lapsed Catholics still believe in God beyond a pleasant nostalgia. Rather, because they have felt the severe, sensuous nature of Catholic belief, they understand what it means to have God absent from that space. In many ways, we might consider the fiction of lapsed Catholics to be a statement of this longing for God, or at least a longing for that forgotten joy of belief.

Longing for an Absent God reveals the meaningful literary differences between lapsed and practicing Catholic writers. The Catholic writers in this book have different styles, methods, and artistic outcomes, but they are all essential contemporary American writers. A direct contrast will help to reveal important differences: a lapsed Catholic, Don DeLillo, compared with a practicing Catholic novelist, Ron Hansen, a deacon in the San Jose Diocese. Both men were raised and educated in the language and intellectual tradition of the Church, and both consider that language and tradition essential to their development as storytellers. They exist within a Catholic literary lineage that can be traced to O'Connor, but they operate in far different styles and modes than her. And, most important, they continue to produce work of the highest merit, lauded by critics both Catholic and secular.

DeLillo's childhood Catholicism, as well as his Jesuit education, has never been secret, but it was not until *Underworld* (1997) that critics began serious examinations of his religious sense, often going back to *White Noise* (1985), DeLillo's novel about Jack Gladney, a professor of Hitler studies at a college in the Midwest. Exposure to an "Airborne Toxic Event" upends his mundane campus life, leading to an act of violent revenge late in the novel.

Wounded, Gladney finds a hospital run by German nuns. A neon cross hangs above the entrance, but these "rustling, ancient" nuns have left God.[16] Gladney, lapsed in his own belief, feels "sentimentally refreshed" when he sees artwork depicting John F. Kennedy and Pope John XXIII together in heaven.[17] He asks the nuns questions, relying on his former faith as a source of knowledge: "You must believe in tradition. The old heaven and hell, the Latin Mass."[18]

The nun's response is a useful metaphor for the continued devotion of lapsed Catholic writers to the vestiges of faith from their youth. She explains that they pretend to believe because "nonbelievers need the believers. They are desperate to have someone believe."[19] The world, the nun asserts, needs not merely religion, but the faithful. They might be called "fools, idiots, those who hear voices, those who speak in tongues."[20] The nun begins speaking "litanies, hymns, catechisms. The mysteries of the rosary perhaps."[21] She taunts Gladney "with scornful prayer," but he does not feel despair: "The odd thing is I found it beautiful."[22] Those who do not believe, DeLillo's novel suggests, often find comfort in faith's power to offer story and meaning to the world. These skeptics are perhaps like Don DeLillo.

DeLillo's constant literary tension has been between the man in the crowd and the man alone in a room. "The future belongs to crowds,"[23] he has said, and television is the "crowd broken down into millions of small rooms."[24] DeLillo's Jesuit education prepared him "to be a failed ascetic" in those rooms.[25] In interviews, he prefers the word religion to faith or belief. He finds religion interesting "as a discipline and a spectacle, as something that drives people to extreme behavior."[26] A cradle Catholic, he was fascinated that "the ritual had elements of art to it and it prompted feelings that art sometimes draws out of us. I think I reacted to it the way I react today to theater. Sometimes it was awesome, sometimes it was funny."[27] When discussing his Catholic experience, DeLillo returns to the contrast between the failed ascetic alone in a small room examining religion rather than practicing faith, and the nameless body in the crowd, a secular congregation of souls.

Underworld, with its cross-tipped church cover and Catholic subplot and climax, compels readers to think about God. The novel's climax is DeLillo's version of a miracle. The vision of a murdered homeless girl appears on a city billboard. Train headlights "sweep the billboard and [Sister Edgar] hears a sound from the crowd."[28] Before the nun sees the girl's face, she "feels the words before she sees the object. . . . This is how a crowd brings things to single consciousness."[29] The billboard is an advertisement for orange juice, and women hold "babies up to the sign, to the flowing juice, let it bathe them in baptismal balsam and oil."[30]

Sister Edgar's miracle is more explanation than dramatization; the work of a man for whom religion has become more dogma than faith. After the visions of the girl disappear, DeLillo offers a proper postmodern elegy:

> And what do you remember, finally, when everyone has gone home and the streets are empty of devotion and hope, swept by river wind? Is the memory thin and bitter and does it shame you with its fundamental untruth—all nuance and wishful silhouette?

> Or does the power of transcendence linger, the sense of an event that violates natural forces, something holy that throbs on the hot horizon, the vision you crave because you need a sign to stand against your doubt.[31]

Although DeLillo claims to have slept through his years at Cardinal Hayes High School, the old stories and rhythms have found their way into the language of his fiction.

Despite *Underworld*'s miracle and the underlying Catholicism of DeLillo's short fiction, *End Zone*, his second novel, is the book that best reveals DeLillo's cultural Catholicism. A metafictional satire about college football, the novel tricks readers into accepting its antithesis: that football is war. DeLillo actually constructs a loose syllogism: football is language, and language is war, and thus football is a form of war. The novel spans one season of the Logos College football team. Emmett Creed, a former fighter pilot now "famous for creating order out of chaos," coaches the team.[32] He fits the formality of his namesake, fully confident that simplicity and rigor will allow him to create a romantic form of masculine asceticism for his team. Practices are held on a field surrounded by canvas blinds; Creed watches the players from atop a tower. Nightly prayer is required on the west Texas campus.

Gary Harkness, a journeyman running back, narrates the novel. He seeks "oneness with God or the universe."[33] He transferred from Penn State after an assistant coach explained that people "don't go to football games to see pass patterns run by theologians."[34] Gary's faith is idiosyncratic, his piety malleable. His thoughts of God evolve into obscenities of sex and death, and the vacillations occur enough in the novel that he resembles a gridiron St. Anthony: "we were in the middle of nowhere, that terrain so flat and bare, suggestive of the end of recorded time, a splendid sense of remoteness firing my soul."[35]

Gary finds pleasure in the "daily punishment on the field."[36] He finds peace in "simple calisthenics, row upon row of us, bending, breathing and stretching, instructing our collective soul in the discipline necessary to make us one body."[37] The Ignatian tradition sings through those lines. Part of the puzzle of reading DeLillo is discerning between his satire and seriousness; for a Jesuit-trained writer, those modes are not mutually exclusive. In DeLillo, much as in James Joyce, the sacred and the profane exist on the same wavelength, separated mostly by perception. Both writers created characters and works that subvert and critique the religion, while also revealing a distinct nostalgia for their lost faith. College students, for DeLillo, are the perfect cast to capture sentimentality and silliness.

The best athlete on the team is a transfer from Columbia. Taft Robinson is the first black student enrolled at Logos, but he quickly rejects the gaze of a "white father watching me run."[38] He quits, and retires to his dorm; an apt representation of the man in "small rooms" that DeLillo so admires. Gary visits Taft to recruit him back on the team, promising that football delivers "what money can't buy."[39] Taft's response: "You mean the crowd."[40] Taft rejects the request. He has made peace with Creed, whose health deteriorates throughout the novel. As Creed moves from body to soul, the season ends, and the team, except for Taft, plays pickup games in the snow, where they "were getting extremely basic, moving into elemental realms, seeking harmony with the weather and the earth."[41]

At Logos College, language is God. Coach Creed implies that football is the perfect form of language, where sign and signified are the closest, but DeLillo punctures that thesis. A motivational sign put in Gary's bedroom loses its efficacy as words become pictures, a rhythmic chant. Another player on the Logos team is "memorizing Rilke's ninth Duino Elegy in German, a language he did not understand. It was for a course he was taking in the untellable."[42] DeLillo's characters seek a perfect language in which ritual transcends language—yet their search is more struggle than reward.

Gary's visit with Taft ends with the reclusive star laughing "quietly into the newspaper between his knees, preparing in his own way for whatever religious act was scheduled to follow."[43] Gary went to Taft seeking answers, but he realizes that Taft's transformation is the result of a journey, one that Gary might never understand. Taft talks about the "degrees of silence"[44] in his room; how he plays the radio, and then stops it: "It becomes a spiritual exercise. Silence, words, silence, silence, silence."[45]

Fascinated, and yet also confused, Gary seeks something beyond language and symbol: he seeks God. His final attempt to reach the divine is through fasting, and the novel ends with his bodily transformation: "High fevers burned a thin straight channel through my brain. In the end they had to carry me to the infirmary and feed me through plastic tubes."[46] Gary's journey from physical to spiritual form reflects Jesuit paleontologist Pierre Teilhard de Chardin's theory of an evolutionary apex of consciousness. In Teilhard's complex, visionary idea, evolution is a process that leads toward convergence. The universe's "enormous layers . . . must somewhere ahead become involuted to a point which we might call *Omega*, which fuses and consumes them."[47]

One of the mandatory courses at Fordham while DeLillo was enrolled was titled "Alpha and Omega."[48] DeLillo explains his perception of Teilhard's point of convergence, the Omega Point, as a next phase of being, "either a paroxysm or something enormously sublime and unenvisionable."[49] This is the metaphysical language of a cultural Catholic but not necessarily a believer.

End Zone is an engagement of the Catholic milieu through the mind of a fond skeptic. In the same way that DeLillo loves the sport of football that he also mocks, his fiction returns to God with intellectual and mystical fascination. The team's workouts are a spiritual exercise for Gary: "I became elated. My body surged and dropped; my mind repeated the process. The indifferent drift of time and all things filled me with affection for the universe."[50] The team is a congregation; these men, together, are a variation of the Catholic communal sense. When the season ends and they scrimmage in the snow, the profluent syntax of DeLillo's sentences feel like a secular creed: "We kept playing, we kept hitting, and we were comforted by the noise and brunt of our bodies in contact, by the simple physical warmth generated through violent action, by the sight of each other, the torn clothing, the bruises and scratches, the wildness of all fourteen, numb, purple, coughing, white heads solemn in the healing snow."[51]

DeLillo's lapsed Catholic worldview in *End Zone*, *White Noise*, and *Underworld* results in a formidable, unique literary aesthetic: a postmodern priest. Armed with the rhetorical flourish and the complex, ambiguous language of Catholic liturgy—and yet divorced of allegiance to its theological sources—DeLillo's prose carries the power of tradition with the freedom of individual thought. DeLillo's literary Catholicism is all stained glass: beautiful artifice, ornamentation in place of lived belief.

Born eleven years after DeLillo, Ron Hansen also attended Jesuit high school and college. Although he grew up in Omaha, Nebraska, Hansen experienced the same Latin Mass as DeLillo, even using the same word, theater, to describe the ceremony. Priests performed Mass for the lay audience, which was observant rather than participatory. Hansen, like DeLillo, recalls that the twin separations between language and symbol, and between celebrant and congregation, complicated meaning but did not neuter experience. When Hansen played the part of Luke the evangelist in a Christmas pageant, he recited "sentences I didn't fully understand,"[52] filled with "fascinating and archaic words."[53] He was struck by the majesty of ceremony. In word and in deed, Latin Mass was a pleasant confusion. He remembers one "parishioner strolling around the church lighting votive candles, oblivious to the Consecration even as the shaken bells heralded it."[54]

Mass elevated the power of narrative for Hansen, showing him that story was an essential element of life. Although Hansen attended daily Mass, his earliest novels were not explicitly Catholic. A discerning reader might glean the Catholic hue to *Desperadoes* or *The Assassination of Jesse James by the Coward Robert Ford*, but only later did Hansen "find the need and confidence to face the great issues of God, faith, and right conduct more directly."[55] *Mariette in Ecstasy* fits that bill.

In 1906, Mariette Baptiste, a seventeen-year-old postulant, is the talk of the Sisters of the Crucifixion convent. Although their days are scheduled down to the minute—silence, recitation, meditation, prayer, work, meals—the sisters can't help but talk about the new, rich teenager in their midst. Why did she join them? What's her secret?

A rare book lauded by both *The Village Voice* and diocesan newspapers, Hansen's novel is written in gorgeous sentences that combine meticulous material specificity with ambiguous emotion. Mariette's room in the convent is described as a "cell" where a "holy water stoup is next to the doorjamb, and just a few feet above Mariette's pillow is a hideous Spanish cross and a painted Christ that is all red meat and agony."[56] The novel captures the marriage of the sacred and the sexual, the pious and the secular.

Hansen introduces readers to these idiosyncratic, devoted sisters, who consider it their "sweet obligation to pray."[57] Many sisters are skeptical of Mariette, but some embrace her, inviting her to their hiding place in the campanile, where one sister says "we're being bad."[58] They talk of old boyfriends, "about what we miss. Whiskers. Dancing. Everything."[59] They talk of God, who sustains them, and Mariette begins to feel at home. Her peace does not last long.

A deeply devout book colored by sex and suspense, *Mariette in Ecstasy* was praised in all corners. *Entertainment Weekly* gave it an "A+," calling it "an astonishing novel, maybe even a great one," a book that is "slender, meditative, exquisitely crafted."[60] At *The New York Times*, Michiko Kakutani praised the book as a "luminous novel that burns a laser-bright picture into the reader's imagination, forcing one to reassess the relationship between madness and divine possession, gullibility and faith, sexual rapture and religious ecstasy," concluding that one need not be Catholic "to be moved and amazed by this fable."[61] It is a novel about the passions of Mariette's body: the "intense, almost erotic fervor that can overtake a young believer."[62]

Good Catholic storytelling has always been corporal, messy, strange, and steeped in the sins of real people. I'm not talking about church thrift-store fare, devotional tales with covers of sunrises over mountains. Consider the profane piety of the whiskey priest in Graham Greene's *The Power and the Glory*, who wanders through a state where Catholicism has been outlawed, offering clandestine penance to believers while indulging in alcohol. The lust of Obadiah Elihue Parker in Flannery O'Connor's "Parker's Back," whose tattooed body began as a place of sexuality, but then becomes a canvas of devotion for his religious wife. The scarred and scorned bodies searching for meaning in the novels of Toni

Morrison. Catholics go for crucifixes over crosses. They want their Mass wine in a chalice, not Solo cups. The Eucharist is not mere symbol; it is substance.

That's a theology a fiction writer can appreciate. *Mariette in Ecstasy* might appeal to disbelievers with a postmodern palate. Either God is real, and therefore the strangest story ever told, or God's unreality makes for absurd performance. Whatever the truth, earnest faith—in which characters love, hate, sin, and struggle in a world where evil is as palpable as the transubstantiated Christ—makes for fascinating entertainment. Hansen's story arrives in truncated yet lyric sentences. Section breaks slice the narrative into vignettes. Ambiguity is not only its theme; it is the book's operating principle.

"Don't try to be exceptional," the nuns warn Mariette, "simply be a good nun."[63] Easier prayed than done. Before Mariette left her father's house for the convent, she stood in her bedroom, dropped her nightgown to the floor, and said, "*Even this I give You.*"[64] She tells one sister that she has "been praying to be a great saint . . . I'll try to be irresistible."[65] When the sisters tell a story about watching a couple kiss in a nearby field, Mariette "smiles tauntingly" and says, "You don't suppose it was me, do you?"[66] Mariette tries to be pious and quiet, but she attracts rumors and concerns. In the eyes of the judgmental sisters, her venial sins include her appearance and her youth; her mortal sin is the stigmata that tattoos her palms and feet.

Hansen doesn't play cheap here. He asks readers to follow belief toward its logical conclusion. If the sisters of the convent seek Christ, they must be ready to receive him in their midst. They are not. They are petty. They want a God for the mind but not the body. That, it seems, would eliminate the mystery and neuter their theology.

Of all the vessels to choose, the sisters wonder, why would God select Mariette? The novel answers that her body, and likely her soul, is ready to receive the ecstasy. Since she was thirteen, Mariette prayed to know Christ's passion. She is now given her chance. A sister finds Mariette kneeling on the floor of her room, "unclothed and seemingly unconscious as she yields up one hand and then the other just as if she were being nailed like Christ to a tree."[67] Later, her "wet blue eyes are overawed as she stares ahead at a wall and she seems to be listening to something just above her, as a girl might listen to the cooing of pigeons."[68]

The novel is part horror, part suspense story. Mariette's actual sister, the convent's Vassar-educated Mother Céline, is dying. "You're my sister, but I don't understand you," Céline says to Mariette.[69] "You may be a saint. Saints are like that, I think. Elusive. Other. Upsetting."[70] Mariette is an object of devotion and envy. Sister Emmanuelle, an older nun, watches Mariette during Compline so that she may "discreetly adore the new postulant in her simple night-black habit and scarf. She's as soft and kind as silk. She's as pretty as affection."[71] While Mariette sleeps, a different sister comes to her bed and kisses Mariette's palm before licking the blood inside the wound. "I have tasted you. See?"[72]

There is no sex in *Mariette in Ecstasy*, but the novel's sexuality—and I do mean sexuality, not merely sensuality—is tied to its sacredness. Mariette's Catholicism is not conjecture; it is lived and livid. Her faith is her skin, her mouth, her desire. Her faith is charged with the closeness of her sin. Mariette has offered her body to God. Someone, or something, has chosen to make that body into a canvas: "Blood scribbles down her wrists and ankles and scrawls like red handwriting on the floor."[73] She becomes a scandal. She leaves red footprints on the floor. She "holds out her blood-painted hands like a present and she smiles crazily" while saying "Oh, look at what Jesus has done to me!"[74] Hundreds of lay people flock to Mass with gifts. They long for a show, but she merely kneels before the priest to receive the Eucharist as "tears of shame and penance shiver like hot mercury in her eyes."[75] Disappointed, the masses leave to long for other miracles, but first one woman "squats to reach through the railing and take back her jar of quince marmalade."[76]

Elusive, other, upsetting, Mariette might be a saint. Her body, though, is not her own. After her stigmata becomes news, a physical examination is scheduled with her father, a well-known local doctor. He is the most dogmatic character in the book, more severe than the old-fashioned sisters. Mariette thinks back to her cold years at home, when her father would drone about "human biology as the dinner plates were cleared."[77] She remembers "how his hard white shirt cuffs would often be brownly spotted with some patient's blood."[78] Mariette has been denied, disbelieved, and even assaulted within this book, but her father's censure stings the most: "You have all been duped," he says.[79] She never recovers from her father's judgment.

A lapsed Catholic might create the same ambiguity as Hansen—in which God's presence in our material world is strange, dizzying, perhaps terrifying and uncomfortable. The performances of lapsed and practicing Catholic writers can be very similar. But sentence to sentence, sound to sound, their outcomes differ. Deep in the text of Hansen's novel, the reader notices that Hansen's prose feels possessed with the ecstasy of Mariette's wounds. This is more than a novel; it is a postmodern prose-poem, written by the hand of a believer. The book is a literary prayer. Mariette's relationship with Christ is not merely spiritual, it is physical and violent in its immediacy. Her passion for God does not belong in this convent, a place where God is a distant source, not a living force.

Mariette is removed from the convent, and returns to the domestic life she lived with her father. Hansen fast-forwards the narrative to 1937. Mariette has never married. Nearly fifty years old, she still prays the hours, honors her vows, and attends Mass at sunrise. In a letter to the current prioress on Easter Vigil, she admits "and yet sometimes I am so sad."[80] She feels a great silence, the stares of children who knew her past secrets, but "Christ still sends me roses. We try to be formed and held and kept by him, but instead he offers us freedom."[81] The novel ends without a scientific resolution of truth, but Hansen appeals to another authority. This is a book by a believer, a man who finds that the true evil of the story is the order's assumption that God only touches us from afar and will never again walk in our midst.

DeLillo and Hansen are neither darlings of readers wishing for fully atheistic writing or those craving purely devotional work. Yet, their shared Catholic identities and literary methods are radically different. For DeLillo the miraculous is artifice. His fiction attempts to manipulate the mysteries of God, to label signs. For Hansen, God is mysterious and complicated, resistant to control. In matters of literature, intellect can neuter faith. DeLillo, the skeptic, is more of a dogmatist than Hansen, the believer. DeLillo's fiction seeks to explain; the miracle in *Underworld* feels manipulative rather than natural. When the characters in *End Zone* arrive at spiritual tran-scendence, it is because their coach and professor have constructed an elaborate ruse for them—God through a game. Hansen's fiction seeks without needing answers. Mariette is haunted by Christ in the same way as readers of the novel are haunted by unanswered, painful questions about love and God's absence.

Hansen became a deacon in the Catholic Church in 2007. His parish is St. Joseph of Cupertino in California. He leads a Bible study group on the Gospel and a Christian film discussion group.

He teaches at Santa Clara University and continues to write historical fiction, including *A Wild Surge of Guilty Passion*, the true crime story of an affair that leads to murder, which then leads to execution by electric chair. *Mariette in Ecstasy* demonstrates what fiction by a skilled practicing Catholic looks like: a fiction where the oddities of piety permeate down to a story's syntax and soul.

The earnest Catholic fiction of Myles Connelly's *Mr. Blue*—even when placed next to the work of a practicing Catholic such as Hansen—feels like a pleasant fossil. Both are practicing Catholic writers, but their differences suggest an evolution of Catholic storytelling, a more malleable understanding of values and ethics within a Catholic worldview. *Longing for an Absent God* will show how the tension and interplay between lapsed and practicing American Catholic writers has formed and sustained a unique and significant literary aesthetic. The powerful literature created by these writers reveals how faith and doubt—and to what extent language can articulate that faith and doubt—teaches us about what it means to be alive.

1

THE HALF-HEARTED AND THE CORRUPT

Graham Greene and Flannery O'Connor

"For writers it is always said that the first twenty years of life contain the whole of experience—the rest is observation," reflects the narrator of Graham Greene's novel *The Comedians*.[1] At twenty, Greene was completing his undergraduate studies at Balliol College, Oxford, and writing for the college's magazine, the *Oxford Outlook*. His essay "The Average Film" appeared in the February 1925 issue. The review itself is forgettable, but its publication would start a series of events that changed Greene's life.

Greene begins his review with an oversimplification: "We either go to Church and worship the Virgin Mary or to a public house and snigger over stories and limericks."[2] A throwaway line in a review that he wrote "in a frightful hurry," but one that did not go unnoticed.[3] Vivien Dayrell-Browning, a secretary for the publisher Basil Blackwell, who had recently released Greene's chapbook of poems, was miffed by the essay. She corrected Greene that Catholics *venerate*, rather than *worship*, Mary. "I most sincerely apologise," Greene wrote to her. "Will you forgive me, and come and have tea with me as a sign of forgiveness?"[4]

Greene turned twenty-one that October. Appropriate to his fictional narrator's claim about age, he went from Protestant experience to observation of the Catholic Church that November. His spiritual curiosity came not from the mind, but from a stirred heart. Greene was in love. Before Vivien, "religion went no deeper than the sentimental hymns in the school chapel."[5] He believed "in nothing spiritual," merely inheriting the Anglican faith of his parents.[6] He had attended chapel at the Berkhamsted School where his father was headmaster. But Vivien's rebuttal to his review intrigued him: "I was interested that anyone took these subtle distinctions of an unbelievable theology seriously."[7] At first, faith was an entertainment for Greene. It was not to be taken seriously. He wanted to marry Vivien, and she did not want to marry a Protestant. A convert herself, Vivien was an ardent believer and convincing enough to stir Greene's curiosity. He finally decided to learn "the nature and limits of the beliefs she held."[8]

The *nature* and *limits*: an appropriately Greene construction. While walking his dog one November day, Greene pondered how Nottingham's Church of St. Barnabas Cathedral held "a certain gloomy power because it represented the inconceivable and the incredible."[9] He dropped a note into an inquiry box, requesting theological instruction, and then went home "to my high tea of tinned salmon."[10] God seemed distant. Impossible.

A week later, he was back at the cathedral to learn about the theology of the church, but not to believe in its faith. His instructor had a literary name: Father Trollope. A former actor, the priest's bookshelves were lined with plays strewn among books of theology. The two men spoke an hour or two a week about the

Gospels and early Christian texts. Greene enjoyed their talks, but remained skeptical. "It was on the ground of a dogmatic atheism that I fought and fought hard," he later reflected.[11] "It was like a fight for personal survival."[12] Greene believed that Jesus Christ existed, but doubted God.

He lost that battle in January 1926. "I became convinced of the probable existence of something we call God," he admits.[13] Not because of philosophy or theology; it was something else. A little wry and a lot stubborn, Greene never quite explains why. That might be the point: against the shore of intellectual skepticism, the tide of belief arrived, gently, but firmly.

Greene was fully received into the Church the next month, and labored over his first confession, a time when "a convert really believes in his own promises."[14] Greene felt a melancholy optimism. Ever sardonic, he still was in awe of the possibility of God, and seemed fascinated by how faith might shape his perception. Following in Catholic tradition, Greene took the name of St. Thomas when baptized, making it clear that he meant Thomas the doubting apostle, not Thomas Aquinas. He left the cathedral full of "somber apprehension," bereft of joy.[15] The world seemed uncertain. He went back "to the Nottingham Journal office and football results and the evening of potato chips."[16] Such flippancy is a manner of personality for Greene. He had entered the Church not fully through the door of intellect, nor fully through the route of faith, but through the gate of mystery.

Greene retained that mystery, that sense of doubt, his entire life. He identified as a Catholic agnostic, and that paradox is telling. When Greene was a Protestant, religion was distant. Religion was merely culture; he had no earnest belief. When Greene became a Catholic, culture became religion and religion became culture. This is not to say that for other Protestants culture and religion do not coexist, but Greene was not a pious Protestant. The distinction is significant: whatever one's variation of Catholicism, it is an encompassing faith. Mass is a cultural event that extends into one's home through domestic practices of piety: crucifixes, votive candles, rosaries, and prayer cards. Once Greene became a Catholic, he was a Catholic everywhere, and always.

"If one is Catholic," Greene explained, "he doesn't have to try to be 'Catholic.'" On the page, "everything that he says or writes inevitably breathes Catholicism."[17] Greene confessed his sins to a priest in a dark cathedral, and then went to the newspaper office to watch sports and eat food. For a Catholic, those juxtapositions were natural, even normal. Greene said he was much like Aunt Augusta in his novel *Travels with My Aunt*. She affirms her Catholicism but adds, "I just don't believe in all the things they believe in."[18] Greene's doubt sustained his faith.

Greene's fiction, and his worldview, were a mixture of satire and sentimentality. He didn't like "conventional religious piety," and preferred the "Catholicism of Catholic cultures"—meaning countries other than England.[19] It might seem like a strange statement, but it underscores that in Greene's theological vision, Christ is more important and tangible than God. For Greene, God was a "mystery, an inexplicable force," so it was better, more concrete, to address Christ in prayer.[20] He preferred crucifixes over crosses. He needed flesh.

Greene found it in Mexico. He'd been commissioned to write a book on religious persecution, specifically the brutal anti-Catholic laws imposed by its governor, Tomás Garrido Canabal. The trip transformed Greene. His faith had been largely intellectual, yet "in Mexico, seeing persecution and attending secret Masses, I found my emotions touched."[21] In England, Greene wryly reveled in being part of the Catholic minority. In Mexico,

Catholics were made the minority through persecution; he called them underdogs. Their passionate piety charged him with the grandeur of Christ among us.

In 1938, Greene traveled to Tabasco, where he "witnessed the fervor of the peasants, who would go back and forth on their knees across the flagstones of those churches in Chiapas."[22] Priests caught celebrating Mass were jailed or shot. Crouching in half-collapsed buildings, priests whispered Mass in secret. Hushed retreats were held in private homes, where congregants would hold "their arms outstretched as though crucified."[23] Those believers, for Greene, were the religion.

Repressed, yet dogged in their belief, Mexican Catholics revealed the power of the Catholic story to Greene. *The Lawless Roads*, his nonfiction account of that time in Mexico, reads like notes for his masterful novel, *The Power and the Glory*. Greene called the novel his "best book by quite a long head."[24]

In the world of Greene's 1940 novel, it's a bad time to be a Catholic. The book's hero is an unnamed priest on the run from Mexican authorities after a state governor has ordered the military to dismantle all vestiges of the religion. Churches are burned. Relics, medals, and crosses are banned. The price for disobedience is death. While many priests give up their beliefs and accept their government pensions, the unnamed priest travels in secret, celebrating Mass and hearing confessions under the cover of night. Yet he's also a gluttonous, stubborn, and angry man drowning in vices, and the religious ambition of his earlier years has been replaced with a constant desire to drink, hence Greene's term for him: the "whiskey priest." Tired of risking his life, the priest even prays to be caught.

A violent, raw novel about suffering, strained faith, and ultimate redemption, *The Power and the Glory* received literary acclaim, but not without catching the attention of Vatican censors. Cardinal Pizzardo, Secretary of the Holy Office, criticized the novel's "unrestrained portrayal of immoral conduct."[25] The cardinal argued that although it is "admirable" to present a Catholic way of life in fiction, "it can never be justified as a means to that end the inclusion of indecent and harmful material."[26]

The Church's rebuke was short-lived. Greene's dark novel and its deeply flawed protagonist offer a richer way to think of faith and self-reflection, one that many Christians might find more accessible and realistic than idealized narratives about belief. In life and in fiction, Greene was more interested in sinners than saints, and the whiskey priest is no saint, at least not for most of the story. If anything, he's closer to the modern conception of the antihero. His pride swells his sense of importance. In one village, where the faithful fear retribution from military officers, the priest hesitates to leave: "Wasn't it his duty to stay, even if they despised him, even if they were murdered for his sake, even if they were corrupted by his example?"[27] Later, he's selfish, crude, and heretical in one stroke: he eats a sugar cube that he discovered by a dead child's mouth, rationalizing, "If God chose to give back life, couldn't He give food as well?"[28] In these and countless other examples, Greene shows how easily dogma can disappear in the face of desperation.

But beneath the darkness of the priest's actions is faith, which he bears witness to in a pivotal scene. Arrested for possessing outlawed alcohol, he's thrown into a small jail cell with a "pious woman," who later notices a couple having sex in the corner. "The brutes, the animals!" she exclaims.[29] And yet the priest counsels the woman to not think that the couple's activity is ugly, "Because suddenly we discover that our sins have so much beauty."[30] In lines that reflect the lived truth of the struggles of faith, the priest explains, "Saints talk about the beauty of suffering. Well, we are not saints, you and I. Suffering to us is just ugly. Stench and crowding and pain. *That* is beautiful in that corner—to them."[31] Greene's aversion to sentimentality makes for palpable theology. He finds God in dirt and in blood—in the Christian struggle to make faith matter in life.

The Power and the Glory encapsulates Greene's Catholic imagination: as a British convert and as a man skeptical of the machinations of the Church. Whereas a more optimistic believer might have written a devotional novel, Greene's novel feels inundated by the messy reality of lived belief. Not despite but *because* of his sins, the whiskey priest is the prototypical Catholic antihero. In Greene's Catholic vision, faith is as much a crutch as it is an antidote; faith is a salve to endure evil, and yet evil remains in the world.

Dramatizing the Christian struggle between doubt and faith, complacency and reflection, Greene's novel examines what happens when a flawed believer is made responsible for the well-being of an entire community. Because the government has destroyed the physical artifacts of Catholicism, the priest must turn inward and confront his own doubts. As the only remaining face of the church, he's forced to air his private demons. But rather than reveling in these sins, the priest is crushed by their significance and seeks to replace greed with grace. "It was too easy to die for what was good or beautiful," the priest reflects, before the novel's tragic end.[32] The world "needed a God to die for the half-hearted and the corrupt."[33] It's the novel's empathy for "the half-hearted and the corrupt"— and its recognition that those people are worthy of salvation—that makes the story uniquely powerful.

That power comes from Greene's development of dramatic story. In Greene's Catholic fictions, which also include novels like *The Heart of the Matter* and *Brighton Rock*, faith informs, but follows, story. Greene was realistic. He knew "any author writing strictly for a Catholic audience would not reach a large public."[34] To write strictly for Catholics would mean to lean heavily on theology, or to have dogma do the exclusive work of plot and character. "If you excite your audience first," Greene explained, "you can put over what you will of horror, suffering, truth. . . . By exciting the audience I mean getting them involved in the story. Once they are involved they will accept the thing as you present it."[35]

As an English, Protestant-raised, Catholic convert, Greene had a unique viewpoint, one that he trained on American fiction and culture. Around the time that *The Power and the Glory* was published, Greene reviewed Conrad Aiken's novel *A Heart for the Gods of Mexico* for *The Spectator*. Greene lamented the state of fiction in America.

He skewers Aiken's novel, concluding that his book contains "what is wrong all the time with the Great American Novel—the inability to see life in any shape at all, whether religious or political."[36] Years later, Flannery O'Connor would agree with Graham Greene about American fiction writers and religion. In 1961, she lamented that American Catholic writers "seem just to be producing pamphlets for the back of the Church."[37] Ironically, two Catholic writers—Walker Percy and J.F. Powers—would win the National Book Award in fiction in 1962 and 1963. Evelyn Waugh, the satirical British novelist and Catholic convert, praised Powers as "almost unique in his country as a lay writer who is at ease in the Church; whose whole art, moreover, is everywhere infused and directed by his Faith."[38] Waugh's perspective mirrored O'Connor's anxieties: American Catholic writing, with Powers as an exception, felt provincial and marginal. She even worried about being "brought up in the novena-rosary tradition . . . you have to save yourself from it someway or dry up."[39]

More skeptical than sentimental, Greene remained the exemplar of the Catholic fiction O'Connor longed to see in her own country. Greene was a first-rate stylist; a sharp mind whose novels valued story over idea and argument. Greene's provocative books were never heretical. His Catholic fiction provided a model for American writers of faith and doubt because he found the two modes inextricable. Greene's characters, including the whiskey priest, feared that God would abandon them. They sinned through their tears. By understanding the power and transcendence of Greene's Catholic vision of storytelling, we can better appreciate the rise of Catholic fiction in America.

Flannery O'Connor first read "all the Catholic novelists, Mauriac, Bernanos, Bloy, Greene" during her graduate years at Iowa.[40] After school, she remained interested in Greene's work, and his Catholic identity. She found the Spring 1954 issue of *Thought*, published by Fordham University, which included an essay that examined *The Power and the Glory*. In a November 1955 letter to Betty Hester:

> I admire her [Elizabeth Sewell] but all through the piece my sympathy goes out to Mr. Greene, or his carcus, which has to suffer this lady-like vulture dining off him. What I feel I suppose is that she is right without much effort but that he is the one sweating to bring something to birth. . . . I haven't read Greene lately enough to know what I think of him. I don't know whether pity is the beginning of love or the corruption of it, or whether it is harder to love something perfect or something feeble.[41]

O'Connor would again reference the critical essay in a January 1957 letter to Maryat Lee, saying it was the "best thing I ever read on Greene . . . [the critic] allowed that [Greene's] sensibility was different from his convictions, the former being Manichean and the latter Catholic. . . . What he does, I think, is try to make religion respectable to the modern unbeliever by making it seedy. He succeeds so well in making it seedy that then he has to save it by the miracle."[42]

Seedy, but saved by a miracle: an effective tagline for the whiskey priest and other downtrodden characters in Greene's Catholic novels. O'Connor's letter to Lee channels Greene's own observation that his works must transcend the religious skepticism of a secular audience; there is not much distance between his desire to "excite" such an audience and O'Connor's claim that he had to be "seedy" in order to do so.

What might an English, Protestant-raised, reluctant Catholic-convert offer such a cradle Catholic as O'Connor? She wrote: "It has always seemed necessary to me to throw the weight of circumstance against the character I favor. The friends of God suffer, etc. . . . This may be something I learned from Graham Greene . . . or it may just be instinct."[43] There is a difference between instruction, influence, and imitation, as O'Connor explained to John Hawkes:

> As between me and Greene there is a difference of fictions certainly and probably a difference of theological emphasis as well. If Greene created an old lady, she would be sour through and through and if you dropped her, she would break, but if you dropped my old lady, she'd bounce back at you, screaming 'Jesus loves me!' I think the basis of the way I see is comic regardless of what I do with it; Greene's is something else.[44]

O'Connor's comic sense—that the world's absurdities are best understood with a dark sense of humor—was complemented by her sense of distortion: the need to create absurd, exaggerated characters and situations in order to get her "vision across to [a] hostile audience."[45] Her consistent usage of visual metaphors—the way one *sees*, my singular *vision*—matched the visceral, pungent nature of her stories. Although Greene has been esteemed for the theological vision of his novels, O'Connor also cultivated a theological sense in her letters and her nonfiction that informed her stories. Both Greene and O'Connor were religious minorities in their settings; unlike Greene, O'Connor almost exclusively wrote fiction about the Protestants around her.

"One of the awful things about writing when you are a Christian," O'Connor wrote in a 1955 letter, "is that for you the ultimate reality is the Incarnation, the present reality is the Incarnation, and nobody believes in the Incarnation; that is, nobody in your audience. My audience are the people who think God is dead. At least these are the people I am conscious of writing for."[46] O'Connor did write book reviews for her diocesan newspaper, the *Georgia Bulletin*, but she could also be found in the pages of *Esquire, The Kenyon Review, Mademoiselle, Harper's Bazaar*, and the *Partisan Review*. The architecture of her theology was complex—her metaphors, symbols, and allusions—but her performance was direct. Anything else would leave those secular audiences confused and probably a bit annoyed.

O'Connor liked to write about Protestants "because they express their belief in diverse kinds of dramatic action which is obvious enough for me to catch. I can't write about anything subtle."[47] The least subtle tale among her stable of unsubtle stories is "Parker's Back," her final work of fiction. The story demonstrates her peculiar and particular vision of distortion.

"Parker's Back" is the story of a tattoo. Once tattooed, we are aware of our body. Blood bubbles beneath the throbbing pen. While our forms are never clean and blank—most of us are adorned with moles and scars—tattoos are the real revisions of body. O'Connor did not compose the tattoo elements of "Parker's Back" from firsthand experience. The story was built "layer by layer, over several years"; she also consulted George Burchett's *Memoirs of a*

Tattooist.[48] O'Connor ordered the book from the eccentric catalogue of Marboro Books, and the book influenced her "more by the spirit . . . than by the details."[49] She "grasped Burchett's feeling for the tattoo as art" and as a form of self-invention.[50]

O'Connor's lupus likely made her acutely aware of her skin, and the refinement and completion of "Parker's Back" occurred during her strained year of 1964. In April, she "woke up covered head to foot with the lupus rash," and spent nearly a month in the hospital.[51] After "four blood transfusions" and "her weight . . . down about twenty pounds," O'Connor returned to her home in Andalusia and worked on "Parker's Back" concurrent with another short story, "Judgment Day."[52] From July onward she "devoted every inch of her consciousness to her two stories."[53]

It is not surprising that O'Connor's final story would be so concerned with flesh and self. Before seeing "a man in a fair, tattooed from head to foot," Obadiah Elihue Parker "had never before felt the least notion of wonder in himself."[54] Although Parker is at best a lapsed Methodist during the entirety of the story, through the observation of this tattooed performer "flexing his muscles so that the arabesque of men and beasts and flowers on his skin appeared to have a subtle motion of its own," O'Connor hints at a certain spiritual awakening, however muted. O'Connor enjoyed painting her revelations indirectly; "Until [Parker] saw the man at the fair, it did not enter his head that there was anything out of the ordinary about the fact that he existed."[55] The ontology of body art is the same ontology as faith in God.

Parker, of course, got "his first tattoo some time after," and the acquisition is Catholic in its sense of suffering as a route toward transcendence: "It hurt very little, just enough to make it appear to Parker to be worth doing."[56] O'Connor, though, makes it clear that Parker's early body work is not religious in nature or intent.

Parker is consumed with a sense of self, and the painting of his skin is a type of personal revelation, an unearthing of his form. His tattoos create his identity, and are his introduction to Sarah Ruth. When his truck breaks down near her house, he fakes an injury to his hand while checking the engine. Sarah Ruth first admonishes him for taking the Lord's name in vain. She notices his tattoos, and he tries to flirt with her. It doesn't work, and Parker is surprised. Most women like his body art. Although the fair performer's body was a colorful mosaic, a living extension and improvement of the body, Parker's work is "something haphazard and botched."[57] His front "was almost completely covered," but his back was bare. Although the tattoos attracted "the girls he liked," he only wanted tattoos he could observe and appreciate.[58]

While Sarah Ruth may not be such a "girl," she is certainly piqued by the tattoos. From the start, her revulsion appears to hide a veiled curiosity. Her initial misreading of his eagle tattoo as a chicken prefigures her inability to later appreciate his marking of Christ. O'Connor is careful to sketch Sarah Ruth as a fundamentalist caricature: she "insisted that the pictures on the skin were vanity of vanities" and "thought churches were idolatrous."[59] As opposed to Parker's Methodist mother, Sarah Ruth's father "was a Straight Gospel preacher," a jab at the literalist approach.[60] They get married, but Parker thinks that the only way to truly sway Sarah Ruth to appreciate his "pictures" would be a religious tattoo on his back. Both the location and the subject matter are necessary and inevitable.

Parker quickly realizes that his first "religious subject"—a Bible—is far too prosaic.[61] At the tattoo parlor, he's unable to explain his desired tattoo. He responds to the artist's question of "Father, Son, or Spirit" with "Just God . . . Christ. I don't care. Just so it's God."[62] Parker scans the book of sample tattoos and moves past the placated representations of Christ but slows when he reaches the more violent presentations: "One showed a gaunt green dead face streaked with blood. One was yellow with sagging purple eyes."[63] O'Connor was well aware of the pictorial dichotomy within Christianity: while the Protestant Christ is clean and regal, the Catholic Christ is fragmented and suffering, fully corporal, truly a God unto earth. Parker is searching for such a literal representation, and he discovers it with "the haloed head of a flat stern Byzantine Christ with all-demanding eyes."[64]

The tattoo is impossible to complete in one sitting, and the artist stops at midnight. When shown the work in progress, Parker is unable to comprehend Christ, merely seeing "little red and blue and ivory and saffron squares."[65] Parker spends his night at the Haven of Light Christian Mission, where the "only light was from a phosphorescent cross glowing at the end of the room" and he "longed miserably for Sarah Ruth."[66] While it may be a bit too prescriptive to read "Parker's Back" as a strict conversion story, the cross induces Parker to remember a tractor crash in which he almost died, and the result is that he, for all intents and purposes, has now been marked.

Sarah Ruth would never accept a tattoo of Christ on Parker's back. O'Connor knows this, as does the reader. Parker, though, has carved a life through the revision of his body, and this is his best form of communication. When he returns home, Sarah Ruth refuses to open the door: she even says "It ain't nobody I know," either referring to Parker or the image of Christ to which she is so fundamentally opposed.[67] She mistakes the image as an *idol*. Still, her rejection of Parker stings— "God? God don't look like that"—and her accusations are voiced with an Old Testament ring of commandment.[68] She batters Parker with a broom until "large welts had formed on the face of the tattooed Christ."[69] Sarah Ruth rejects the visual Christ because she claims "He's a spirit."[70] Her revulsion, though, is hollow. Parker's marks of faith run much deeper than hers.

The symbolism of "Parker's Back" feels inspired by St. Paul's letter to the Galatians. At the conclusion of the exhortations penned by a scribe, Paul, who is "writing to you in my own hand,"[71] contrasts his interpretation of the Hebrew tradition of circumcision with a most enigmatic pronouncement: "From now on, let no one make troubles for me; for I bear the mark of Jesus on my body."[72] The line has formed a legend for religious tattooists: some have used the reference to laud body art as a way to show belief in Christ.

The nearest translation of Paul's Greek is *stigmata*: scars rather than markings. Whether O'Connor considered the theological subtleties of Paul's line is irrelevant. Her Catholic Church has never made steadfast declarations regarding tattoos, leaving the practice of body art to personal discretion. In that place, between orthodoxy and the world, O'Connor crafts Parker as more than merely an apparition of his Old Testament namesake. Parker is the end of the fundamentalist order: his marks bear the raised freshness of a new tattoo. His wounds are the result of a whipping from the broom, but he bears a most beautiful and permanent wound in the Byzantine form across his back. His story proper ends in tears, but his nexus is that night on a cot, where his stinging back carries the image and icon in which his wife will never truly believe.

"Parker's Back" was first published in the April 1965 issue of *Esquire*. It was O'Connor's second appearance in the magazine. She died a few months before "Parker's Back" was published alongside a pair of articles about Robert F. Kennedy, and new work by Stanley Elkin and Erskine Caldwell. O'Connor had transcended Milledgeville; she had transcended Georgia, her diocese, her anxieties. In her own way, she had brought Graham Greene's brand of Catholic fiction about the half-hearted and the corrupt to America.

2

PRESENT GOD

The Fiction of Walker Percy and Andre Dubus

In the July 1963 issue of *Esquire*, fiction editor Rust Hills caused a stir by publishing "The Structure of the American Literary Establishment: Who Makes or Breaks a Writer's Reputation? A Chart of Power." From F. Scott Fitzgerald to Ernest Hemingway to Joan Didion, *Esquire* published talented writers, but Hills wanted to look at the American literary scene as a whole. The result was a multicolored graphic packed with names, subgroups, and quirky commentary.

Colored orange, "The Hot Center" is an oblong shape that meanders through the list of names, and includes what Hills deemed to be the literary elite: the writers, agents, publishers, and magazines that cultivated literary power in America. Flannery O'Connor was in the red-hot center, along with James Baldwin, Truman Capote, and T.S. Eliot. Hills explained that "in the hot center most of these people know one another, and because they admire one another's work sincerely and are in a position to do something helpful, things get done. Reputations get made."[1] O'Connor was not merely a great writer; she was an essential member of the literary elite.

The "chart of power" was too meticulous, too precise to be merely tongue-in-cheek, and engendered a strong reaction (the *New York Times Book Review* editors did not love being relegated to "Squaresville"). *Esquire* was the type of magazine sold at the grocery store, and O'Connor was amused by the "local reaction" when she appeared in its pages: "You would think that at last I was really going places."[2]

The thought that O'Connor was receiving accolades in that most secular of publications, with its tagline "the magazine for men," feels like the type of comic quip that fellow Southern writer Walker Percy—also included in the power chart although not fully in the red-hot center—would make in one of his interviews or essays.

O'Connor and Percy were mutual admirers. In a March 1963 speech at Sweet Briar College, later published as "Novelist and Believer," O'Connor said "At its best our age is an age of searchers and discoverers, and at its worst, an age that has domesticated despair and learned to live with it happily."[3] Her particular choice of words—*searchers, discoverers, despair*—reflect the language and milieu of Percy's debut novel, *The Moviegoer*. His book won the 1962 National Book Award, and he earned praise from O'Connor. She had observed an American malaise; Percy offered her a cast of characters.

Her first letter to Percy was a succinct gift of praise, saying that she was glad that he "won the Nat'l Book Award. I didn't think the judges would have that much sense but they surprised me."[4] Although they would only meet once, when Percy came to a speech that O'Connor gave in New Orleans, their correspondence cultivated their shared interests and ideals. O'Connor thought Percy captured Southern identity, even though his characters differed from the backwoods world that she herself dramatized.

"What he was saying," O'Connor wrote about Percy's vision, "was that we have had our Fall. We have gone into the modern world with an inburnt knowledge of human limitations and with a sense of mystery which could not have developed in our first state of innocence—as it has not sufficiently developed in the rest of the country."[5] O'Connor appreciated how Percy's fiction had a Catholic moral and cultural sense. She certainly had praise for other Catholic writers, among them J.F. Powers, whose novel *Morte D'Urban* won the 1963 National Book Award; yet, Percy was a fellow Southerner. Here was a writer who was like her, and yet also not.

The novelist Caroline Gordon, who helped first connect the two writers, once told Percy that the main character of *The Moviegoer* "is something like the monks of the third century; where they sought the desert, Jack sought the wasteland of a suburb."[6] O'Connor wrote of revival tents and river baptisms; Percy wrote about sidewalks and offices. They were both misunderstood by their kind. O'Connor's penchant for the violent and grotesque stymied certain Catholic circles, and Percy felt the same way about his own work: "a lot of people think of me as a Catholic writer and yet Catholics think I'm a real nut. So I usually find myself falling somewhere in between .... Non-Catholics put me with Catholics and the Catholics would like to get rid of me."[7]

Orphaned by the suicide of his father and the death of his mother in a car accident, Percy grew up with his cousin, the poet and lawyer William Alexander Percy, in Greenville, Mississippi. Percy felt like he never fit in with old guard Southern writers:

"Faulkner and all the rest of them were always going on about this tragic sense of history, and we're supposed to sit on our porches talking about it all the time. I never did that. My South was always the New South. My first memories are of the country club, of people playing golf."[8] He envisioned Jack "Binx" Bolling of *The Moviegoer* in the same way, "so detached that he is almost unsouthern; I mean he's outside of it, he's outside of the Southern scene."[9]

Percy received his medical degree from Columbia's College of Physicians & Surgeons in 1941. During his residency at Bellevue Hospital, he contracted tuberculosis while performing an autopsy. Percy spent several years recuperating at the Trudeau Sanatorium in the Adirondacks. "I wasn't fighting for my life," he explained. Rather, he was on two years of "enforced idleness," and the bedrest caused him to ponder "what am I doing here, is the rest of my life going to be like this?"[10] Isolation, idleness, and existentialism are proper bedfellows, and Percy cultivated his lifelong interest in philosophy, language, and the modern man's peculiar despair. He read the works of Jean-Paul Sartre and Fyodor Dostoevsky. Once recovered, he returned south, but retained his newfound fascinations.

In 1946, he was in love with Mary "Bunt" Townsend, whom he'd met years earlier in Greenville, but was hesitant about marriage. Percy and his childhood friend, historian Shelby Foote, set out to New Mexico on part road trip, part philosophical sojourn. There Percy made his decision to marry Bunt, and to investigate the Catholic faith, which had interested him since reading the work of Christian philosophers. The latter decision upset the unbelieving Foote; Percy's conversion was surprising.

As an undergraduate, Percy "lived in the attic of a fraternity house with four other guys. God, religion, was the furthest thing from our minds and talk—from mine, at least. Except for one of us, a fellow who got up every morning at the crack of dawn and went to Mass. He said nothing about it and seemed otherwise normal."[11] While at Columbia, Percy was friends with two Catholics who regularly went to Mass and would "hang one of those garish Catholic calendars on the wall. That struck me as outrageous. I was offended by Catholicism. The offense is part of the clue, of course, part of the secret."[12]

Soon after Percy married, his religious curiosity led to action. A visit to Holy Name of Jesus Church led to Percy and his wife's conversion in 1947. He was thirty-one.

Shelby Foote was skeptical of God, and of Percy's conversion, but Percy was a contrarian. What could be more countercultural for a Southerner of humanist ilk to become a Catholic of the Roman variety? "My whole bent is toward black humor and satire," Percy wrote. "Why I should be stuck with the Catholic faith I don't know. It is not convenient."[13] There is a paradox of convenience between his Catholicism and his writing. Percy said he "didn't really begin to write until after I became a Catholic."[14] His earliest, unpublished attempts at fiction were rather devotional and trite—the same type of light Catholic fare that he would later bemoan.

During these years, Percy was moving further in his philosophical readings. He had credited Søren Kierkegaard's essay "The Difference Between a Genius and an Apostle" as being most responsible for his conversion, but now he was reading philosophy *as* a Catholic.

He was publishing short pieces in Catholic periodicals like *Commonweal* and *America*, and theological publications such as *Thought*, Fordham University's quarterly journal. Percy also wrote philosophical treatises. These were not the work of a hobbyist, but rather a capable autodidact. "Symbol as Hermeneutic in Existentialism" appeared in *Philosophy and Phenomenological*

Research, "Symbol, Consciousness, and Intersubjectivity" in *The Journal of Philosophy*, among others.

After scrapping his earlier, unpublished fiction manuscripts, Percy began writing *The Moviegoer* at the same time he was writing his dense philosophical work, but he had the good sense to know a novel is not an exegesis. His first novel was a book of ideas, but the ideas lived. Binx, the novel's protagonist, has a messy philosophy; his method is often unsound. He was the perfect character to live Percy's philosophical quandary: modern man has much, but is unhappy.

"The American novelist traditionally had been thought of as an adventurer in the concrete," Percy wrote, contrasting American and French novelists.[15] He admired Sartre's medium—the idea of "the fiction form as a vehicle for incarnating ideas"—but not his message.[16] Percy agreed that "modern man is deranged," but unlike atheist existentialists, "I write from that premise and ask, What are the options for characters living in a deranged world in which the Church is no longer regnant, no longer even terribly important in many places?"[17]

The crux is that Percy took the Church seriously, even when he was being comedic and profane. He shared that literary style with O'Connor, and in many ways, he inherited her place in the secular literary canon: the Southern Catholic writer who, although he published in *Esquire* and *The Sewanee Review*, remains earnestly devoted to a real, lived faith. After her passing, Percy held up O'Connor as an essential American Catholic writer. He thought O'Connor's sense of distortion was not merely necessary as an act of fiction writing; it was a theological imperative. Percy is the skeptical convert, the writer who was not reared on Catholic schoolboy nostalgia. He was the intellectual Protestant foil, in certain ways, to O'Connor and her lifelong devotion to Catholicism, making his praise of her writing all the more significant.

Percy disliked the word existentialist because it "is being so abused now that it means very little."[18] He had the same disdain for religious vocabulary. "When you speak of religion, it's almost impossible for a novelist because you have to use the standard words like 'God' and 'salvation' and 'baptism,' 'faith,' and the words are pretty well used up. . . . [O'Connor] got around the difficulty through grotesquerie and exaggeration and bizarre writing."[19] The Christian novelist "has to do what [James] Joyce did: he has to practice his art in cunning and in secrecy and achieve his objective by indirect methods."[20] Joyce and O'Connor are curious literary bedfellows, but we get Percy's point: the earnestly religious artist will always be a curiosity, and even the lapsed religious artist must be aware of how past faith leaves marks.

Percy shared O'Connor's affinity for dogma. Like her, he found the Church "liberating. It puts you in touch with, first with the mystery, and that, in truth, religion has to do with mysteries. It addresses the nature of man."[21] Although Percy never shied from identifying as Catholic, he said O'Connor was "militant . . . and was aware of it every minute . . . she's one of the best writers that we have and her faith is certainly an asset, not a defect."[22] More than a peer, O'Connor became a literary saint to Percy, someone heroic and sanctified. A doctor inclined toward diagnosis, he noted that despite the challenges of her lupus, "she pursued her vocation with absolute fidelity."[23] He called her literary lectures "very apostolic," an attempt to "spread the good news."[24]

Percy was a different type of writer. He and O'Connor shared a common truth, but their lives and contrasts so differed that their disparity threatened to make O'Connor into a literary martyr—the Catholic writer who died young, who was more than human. O'Connor's ghost continues to the present: any emerging Catholic writer of fiction is sure to be compared to her. That Percy can be separated from her shadow speaks to the power of his own vision.

That vision arises from a critique of the modern world. "Alienation," Percy claimed, "is nothing more or less than a very ancient, orthodox Christian doctrine. Man is alienated by the nature of his being here. He is here as a stranger and as a pilgrim, which is the way alienation is conceived in my books."[25] Percy envisioned alienation and Christian pilgrimage as linked. Unlike Faulkner, he did not write of "the Snopses or the denizens of Tobacco Road," and unlike O'Connor, he did not write of "half-mad backwoods preachers."[26] He wrote of "the very people who have overcome these particular predicaments and find themselves living happily ever after in their comfortable exurban houses and condominiums."[27]

Enter Binx Bolling, a man whose life is going nowhere. Despite his many faults—sarcastic, chauvinistic, selfish—he has embarked on a spiritual "search" for meaning in the world. And intertwined with that search are nightly pilgrimages to a street theater with a speaker pointed toward the world, to bring in the lapsed and remind them of the magic of the silver screen. Percy captures a liturgy of the cinema, and his scenes about film are just nostalgic enough to make readers long for sticky floors, previews, and the silence that clothes a darkened room.

The first theater described in *The Moviegoer* is nearly empty, "which was pleasant for me but not" for the manager.[28] "A pink stucco cube, sitting out in a field all by itself," wind-whipped waves on nearby Lake Pontchartrain can be heard during the show.[29] Afterward, he talks with the manager while the sidewalk speaker spits movie conversation into the world. Binx is happy "out in the sticks," talking film; his date would rather go out to dinner and dancing.[30]

Binx finds meaning in going to the movies. The Tivoli, his neighborhood cinema, has a marquee that reads: "Where Happiness Costs So Little."[31] It was there that Binx "first discovered place and time, tasted it like okra."[32] Early in the novel, Binx admits that he's an oddball. Good or bad, he just wants to be at the movies. "Other people, so I have read, treasure memorable moments in their lives"—travel, family, love.[33] Not him. "What I remember is the time John Wayne killed three men with a carbine as he was falling to the dusty street in *Stagecoach*, and the time the kitten found Orson Welles in the doorway in *The Third Man*."[34]

For Binx, it is not merely the movie that is important: it is the journey to the theater. The approach, the mood. He describes evening as "the best time": "There are not so many trees and the buildings are low and the world is all sky."[35] Above Lake Pontchartrain "a broken vee of ibises points for the marshes; they go suddenly white as they fly into the tilting salient of sunlight."[36] He keeps walking and watching and cataloging: "Station wagons and Greyhounds and diesel rigs rumble toward the Gulf Coast, their fabulous tail-lights glowing like rubies in the darkening east. Most of the commercial buildings are empty except the filling stations where attendants hose down the concrete under the glowing discs and shells and stars."[37]

The manager of the Tivoli assures Binx that a new film is "a real pleaser," but Binx feels despair, not only from the film itself, but the nearly empty theater, with "only a few solitary moviegoers scattered through the gloom, the afternoon sort and the most ghostly of all, each sunk in his own misery."[38] Yet, there's an odd comfort in this melancholy, in part because Binx knows the melodramatic hue of the theater is a product of the place itself. If we fully allow ourselves to become immersed in a film at the cinema, we are ceding our sense of setting. We are embracing our imagination's power. The cinema that we are in is nothing, it is a vessel, and yet it is therefore our everything.

Binx feels the same way at The Moonlite Drive-In. *Fort Dobbs* is playing. "Gnats swim in the projection light and the screen shimmers in the sweet heavy air. But in the movie we are in the desert."[39] Outdoors or indoors, when we get together to watch a film, we breathe together in performance.

"All movies smell of a neighborhood and a season," Binx says.[40] He remembers "the smell of privet" when he came out of *The Oxbow Incident*, and the "camphor berries popping underfoot."[41] The gnosis of theater is simple, and yet beautiful.

Yet the route of Binx's spiritual search is winding, conflicted, broken. Binx begins the novel twenty-nine years old, having lived in Gentilly, a New Orleans suburb, for the past four years. He's a sarcastic first-person narrator and a proud capitalist. He manages a branch of his uncle's brokerage firm. He subscribes to *Consumer Reports* and buys the top-rated products, including the finest deodorant. He's happy in Gentilly. Percy would consider this contentment a calm sort of alienation, as Binx "lives in a place like Gentilly to savor its ordinariness."[42]

He is content—until he is not. His stoic Aunt Emily sends him a note, wishing to speak to Binx about his stepcousin, Kate. She is not well. Aunt Emily wants Binx to take Kate out and boost her spirits. Make her laugh. Binx, taken to daydreaming, lets his mind wander to his idea of the "search," which begins vaguely existential, but evolves into a religious journey. Binx's mother is Catholic; she is even considered "devout" by the other women in the family. That isn't saying much; for them, devout means "that she is a practicing Catholic."[43]

Binx is "nominally" Catholic because of his mother's faith.[44] Yet, the language and earnestness of his search cuts through the sarcasm of the rest of the novel. Binx is a goof when talking about money and women, but he is serious about the possibility of belief. When he criticizes one character as being "no more aware of the mystery which surrounds him than a fish is aware of the water it swims in," he is using Catholic theological language to describe the world.[45]

When Binx's mother speaks about a family member receiving extreme unction, the Catholic sacrament of the final anointing of the sick, Binx says she "speaks of such matters in a light allusive way, with the overtones of neither belief nor disbelief but rather of a general receptivity to lore."[46] That might be a son's cynical perception of his mother, but Binx develops his sense of his mother's faith even further. He thinks that she "uses" God as "but one of the devices that come to hand in an outrageous man's world, to be put to work like all the rest in the one enterprise she has any use for: the canny management of the shocks of life."[47] Binx doesn't realize that he's describing faith.

Binx's family "would never dream of speaking of religion— raising the subject provokes in them the acutest embarrassment," although they would "argue forty-five minutes about the mechanics of going to Mass."[48] The Catholics Binx knew wouldn't talk about Jesus—"certainly if they spoke to me of God, I would jump into the bayou"—but they would compare the appeal of attending the 9:00 Mass in Biloxi to the 10:30 Mass in Bay St. Louis.[49] They settle on the earlier Mass in Biloxi, at an old, packed church. Binx doesn't receive the Eucharist; instead he watches the service unfold as if it was a movie.

Binx is Percy's consummate pilgrim; he is, quite literally, itinerant through much of the novel. He travels by train to Chicago with Kate. They sleep together, but his euphoria is short-lived.

He hears from Aunt Emily, who is unhappy that Kate has left home. Binx can't placate Aunt Emily, so he and Kate board a bus home. It is the night before Mardi Gras; there are no trains or flights open. When they return, Aunt Emily dresses down Binx for several pages. In an interview, Percy reflected on how the speech was like one he'd hear in his own youth: "You behaved like a gentleman, the Southern honor code, chivalry, grace doing right, treating women with respect. If somebody insults you, then fight. Aren't these the Roman stoic virtues? There's very little said about turning the other cheek."[50]

Aunt Emily's speech is stoic, not Catholic. Dazed, Binx stumbles into his thirtieth birthday. It is Ash Wednesday; he is frustrated. "My search has been abandoned," he says; "it is no match for my aunt, her rightness and her despair, her despairing of me and her despairing of herself."[51] Binx appears to have returned to where he began the novel: in stasis.

Later, Binx sits with Kate in her Plymouth, and they watch Catholics go into the church. Binx is reminded that it is Ash Wednesday; he does not get ashes himself. They speak about Aunt Emily, and their plans for the future. Binx notices a man, "more middle-class than one could believe," enter the church.[52] He and Kate finish their conversation, and then the man exits the church. Binx is unable to tell whether the man has gotten ashes. The black man's skin is "an ambiguous sienna color and pied."[53]

The man returns to his car, and Binx's mind wanders into a philosophical space. "It is impossible to say why he is here," Binx thinks.[54] Is the man's participation in this church a ritual part of entering the middle class? Does the man believe that God is present in that church? "Or is he here for both reasons: through some dim dazzling trick of grace, coming for the one and receiving the other as God's importunate bonus?"[55]

Binx doesn't know. He has spent the novel chasing secretaries, watching movies, and trying to find the meaning of life in some pre-Lenten rush. *The Moviegoer* is not a conversion story. Binx is more open to the mystery and grace of Catholicism, but his search is largely abandoned. He marries Kate; his aunt warms to him. He is no longer in despair.

Rather than conclude with a grand, extended articulation of faith, Percy's novel simmers and settles, perhaps suggesting that faith is most realistically experienced in the background of our daily lives. During his search, Binx sought signs and wonders. What he found was more muted and authentic.

Earlier in the novel, when asked if he would become a godfather to the baby of a fellow Korean War veteran, Binx responds that he doubts he can do so since he is "not a practical Catholic."[56] Percy explained that "there is hardly a moment in my writing when I am not aware of where, say, my main character—who is usually some kind of Catholic bad, half-baked, lapsed, whatever—of where he or she stands vis a vis the Catholic faith."[57] Binx's Catholicism is not a struggle of dogma, but one of love, identity, and doubt. His doubts are more experiential than ecclesiastical. He trusts that his faith is true, but knows that life is unfair.

"In all of Percy's novels Catholicism is essential as an alternative" to the secularism of the modern world—so states a review of *Lancelot*, Percy's fourth novel, in the April 1977 issue of *Harper's* magazine.[58] The reviewer was a Southerner, although he would qualify that identification. Andre Dubus was born in Lake Charles, Louisiana, but grew up in Lafayette, about two hours from Percy's home in Covington. Following a stint in the Marine Corps and an MFA from the University of Iowa, Dubus had already lived in Massachusetts for ten years. He taught at Bradford College and included *The Moviegoer* in a few of his classes.

In his review, Dubus notes that *The Moviegoer* was published when Percy was forty-five. What some readers and critics perceive to be a sense of repetition in his novels is not a deficiency: "what we don't see in Percy's novels is the changing vision of the world that we often get from a writer who publishes while he is young, and then continues to write. With *The Moviegoer* we were in the hands of a mature writer whose themes had already chosen him."[59] Here the passive voice could be a nod toward the mysteries of Percy's conversion, or simply the tendency of Dubus to ascribe a higher power to our earthly foibles.

Whatever the reason, his point is well taken. In Percy's novels, "the hero is searching: he is searching because he has to, because if he does not search he will join the active dead who move about Percy's joyless landscape, making sounds, making money, making children."[60] His search arises from several questions: "What is one to do on an ordinary afternoon? Therefore, what is time for? What is a human being for?"[61] Lofty questions, but necessary questions. Real ones.

In 1983, *Granta* magazine editor Bill Buford coined the term "dirty realism" to describe a new fiction "emerging from America, and it is a fiction of a peculiar and haunting kind."[62] Buford claims this new fiction is distinctly American, but not in the traditional senses. It is not heroic or grand. It is neither experimental nor historical. Instead, this fiction is "devoted to the local details, the nuances, the little disturbances in language and gesture."[63] These were "unadorned, unfurnished, low-rent tragedies about people who watch day-time television, read cheap romances or listen to country and western music."[64] Stories about waitresses, cashiers, and construction workers. Stories about people in trouble. And perhaps most importantly, stories from writers who had mastered the short story form.

Buford devoted an entire issue to these writers: Jayne Anne Phillips, Richard Ford, Raymond Carver, Elizabeth Tallent, Frederick Barthelme, Bobbie Ann Mason, and Tobias Wolff. He says that he wished he had more room to include Mary Robison and Ann Beattie. An impressive lineup of writers, with one glaring omission: Andre Dubus. Dubus's fiction contained all of the elements that Buford praised in his contemporaries: simple yet precise language, troubled but endearing characters, and a disdain for linguistic pyrotechnics that Dubus thought made writers like John Barth and Thomas Pynchon seem pretentious. He'd already published several story collections, including *Separate Flights* (1975), *Adultery and Other Choices* (1977), *Finding a Girl in America* (1980), and *The Times Are Never So Bad* (1983).

Buford must have had his reasons for leaving Dubus off the roster, but Dubus's work existed in a different realm from his contemporaries. He wrote about the same type of character, in the same type of situation, using the same type of language as them. But as a sincere, and often sentimental, Catholic, Dubus put his characters in the context of sin and salvation. Although Wolff and Barthelme were both Catholics, their past or present faith was more in the background. In contrast, Dubus's stories often hinge on theological points. His stories were devotional but never doctrinaire; more so than any other Catholic short story writer in the shadow of Vatican II and its examination of the church in the modern world. Dubus captured a rift that the Council Fathers lamented in *Gaudium et Spes*, a document known as the Pastoral Constitution on the Church in the Modern World: "the dichotomy between the faith which many profess and the practice of their daily lives."[65] For Dubus, that split was just life.

Dubus tried to answer the same questions as Percy in his fiction, but with different results, and a vastly different method. It is tempting to synthesize Dubus, Percy, and O'Connor in some grand unified theory of Southern Catholic literature, but Dubus breaks the formula. Like O'Connor, he was a cradle Catholic, and he did write about violence, but his characters were often working-class Catholics. Their collars were far bluer than those in Percy's fictions. Although he could be self-deprecating in essays and interviews, Dubus was often deadly serious in his fiction. The theological and moral questions pondered in his fiction are considered at the dinner table or in the bedroom, not as abstractions. His characters are real, his plots are real, and even his syntax is real—there is no artifice in his fiction.

Dubus is a Southern writer in a different way than Percy and O'Connor. By his own admission, Dubus "was raised a Catholic in the suburbs of small towns."[66] It wasn't quite the golf courses on which Percy was bred, but it was not O'Connor's backwoods, either. "My 'Southern-ness,'" Dubus explained, "was acquired in college and by reading Douglas Southall Freeman. For years I worked on Southern stories and a novel that was filled with miscegenation and lynching and the like. Then, when I read Camus's *The Plague*, I discovered that I was the guy who was trying to capture the rhythm of the horses' hooves on the Champs Élysées when he had never been there. I was writing about Faulkner's South, not my own life."[67]

Dubus could even be stern about the South: "I can't stand the Southern men I know who are middle class . . . I don't like their irony. I don't like the way they treat women."[68] His fiction is unburdened by regional nostalgia, but that doesn't mean that his work was devoid of the sentimental; it merely had other origins. Those included his Catholic faith, his feelings about the military, and his ideas of fatherhood—perhaps his most endearing, and complex, subject.

He offers insight into that theme in his essay "Digging." At seventeen, weighing "one hundred and five pounds," Dubus was sent to work by his "ruddy, broad-chested father."[69] Dubus didn't want to go. His father, an ex-Marine who carried a .22 on his belt for cottonmouths encountered during his surveying work, had a message for the foreman: "make a man of him."[70]

Dubus describes pickaxing a trench in Lafayette, Louisiana heat. Sunburned and weak, his mouth is dry. He swallows salt tablets and drinks endless water, but later becomes sick and vomits. He does not tell the foreman; he does not want to tell his father. But his father learns, and takes young Dubus to lunch. He buys the boy a pith helmet for the sun. Dubus feels like a fool, but wore it all summer because "I did not want to hurt him."[71] He ends the essay by thanking his father for making him work "instead of taking me home to my mother and sister," where it was comfortable, the air cooled by a fan.[72]

Dubus knows his father "may have wanted to take me home. But he knew he must not, and he came tenderly to me."[73] He made his son a man by letting him know that weakness could be overcome.

Reading Dubus's essays is like entering a rougher world of work and a place where the love between father and son could be expressed in silence. In contrast, Dubus's fiction scratches and tears. His stories document the sexual and violent collisions between men and women. Manipulation, jealousy, and revenge: his fictive men are often terrible. They are shadows of the male archetypes chiseled by his similarly Catholic predecessor, Ernest Hemingway. Ray, the first person narrator of "The Pretty Girl," rapes his ex-wife, Polly. When the narrative leans toward her, Dubus trades first person for third person limited. She realizes that men "need mischief and will even pretend a twelve-ounce can of beer is wicked if that will make them feel collusive while drinking it."[74] Polly's Catholic faith is her comfort. She attends Mass weekly, but "did not receive communion because she had not been in the state of grace for a long time."[75] She had slept with another man during the final months of her marriage and will not even seek the sacrament of confession. The characters in Dubus's fiction believe sins bring immediate and eternal consequences.

Such writing about sin was sometimes met with confusion by secular audiences. O'Connor's distortive fictional sense made her fiction unreal, but Dubus's stories are painfully mundane (he kept a notebook of newspaper articles that he used as the basis for his stories). Dubus was out of place in his literary moment. His only novel, *The Lieutenant*, was published in 1967, the same year that John Barth read "The Literature of Exhaustion" at the University of Virginia, in which he praised the aesthetics and style of post-modernism—a style Dubus hated.

In his introduction to Dubus's essay collection, *Broken Vessels*, Tobias Wolff explains: "[For Dubus], the quotidian and the spiritual don't exist on different planes, but infuse each other. His is an unapologetically sacramental vision of life in which ordinary things participate in the miraculous, the miraculous in ordinary things. He believes in God, and talks to Him, and doesn't mince words."[76] This belief operated in the real, tangible world, where the sacred and profane coexist, as in the story "Sorrowful Mysteries" where the main character's girlfriend is introduced in such a manner: "She likes dancing, rhythm and blues, jazz, gin, beer, Pall Malls, peppery food, and passionate kissing, with no fondling. She receives Communion every morning, wears a gold Sacred Heart medal on a gold chain around her neck."[77]

In his essays, Dubus shows how sacraments "soothe our passage" through life.[78] His daily receipt of the Eucharist means "the taste of forgiveness and of love that affirmed, perhaps celebrated, my being alive, my being mortal."[79] God needed to be brought down to the real, dirty world. Without the "touch" of the Eucharist, "God is a monologue, an idea, a philosophy; he must touch and be touched, the tongue on flesh."[80]

Dubus's visceral Catholicism has led to comparisons with Hemingway—ones he did not shy away from. Hemingway once said he "never wanted to be known as a Catholic writer," that he was content being a "very dumb Catholic" with "so much faith that I hate to examine into it."[81] Certainly his literary representations of Catholicism do little to shed light on his personal faith, leading some readers to question the authenticity of his conversion and, in light of his own mythology and his pared-down stories, view his Catholicism as mere novelty.

Despite these comparisons and Dubus's own admission that Hemingway inspired him, Dubus was his own man on the page and anything but a dumb Catholic. He was comfortable using his faith to articulate a structure for his fiction. If Dubus were a dogmatist, he would lay judgment on the adulterers in his fiction. Rather, writing from a Catholic worldview, he reveals how faith helps and hurts them in equal amounts.

During the first meeting of his courses at Bradford College, Dubus would write a statement on the blackboard: "Art is always affirmative, because it shows we can endure being mortal."[82] Struggle, suffer, endure: Dubus's stories might be sorted into devolutions of love, violent tales of pain and revenge, or meditations on the relationships between fathers and daughters.

The scars of violence are present in "Leslie in California," a brief and underappreciated story. The title character's plain-spoken, first person narration suggests acceptance of her situation. She wakes to the smell of beer; her eye hurts. She counts the discarded bottles and cans, "knowing how many it takes" to be at risk for another black eye from Kevin, her boyfriend.[83] "Hon" is the word he speaks most often in the story, and he promises to never hit her again, but all Leslie sees are weapons: the knife on his belt, the "cooking forks, ice picks, hammers, skillets, cleavers, wine bottles, and I wonder if I'll be one of those women. I think of this without fear, like I'm reading in the paper about somebody else dead in her kitchen."[84] Leslie looks out the window at the surrounding hills, and when Kevin leaves for work, she ruminates about them and the flight she longs for, but is not ready to attempt.

Dubus's stories about fathers and daughters are generally counted among his finest fiction. One such story is "Bless Me, Father," in which a young woman learns her father is having an affair. The woman, Jackie, is nineteen and surrounded by "sin" herself, but besides being "pinned" to her boyfriend and some recreational drinking and smoking, she has done nothing to "interfere with her staying in the state of grace."[85] Dubus winks his way through the story; of course his Catholics are having sex, but they are also experiencing guilt and second thoughts and worry. In Dubus's fiction, faith offers his characters comfort, but also causes them pain: they feel inadequate before God. Rather than judging his characters, Dubus implies that this longing for God makes them human.

"A Father's Story" is Dubus's ultimate exploration of the tenuous distance between man and God. The story is narrated by Luke Ripley, a divorced Catholic in his mid-fifties who never contributes to the Sunday collection because he doesn't "feel right about giving money for buildings, places."[86] He would rather a pared-down church with "no padding on the kneelers."[87] He wants the Vatican to give its money to the poor, but admits that he would not do the same because "being a real Catholic is too hard."[88]

The story begins with a long confessional monologue that documents Luke's normal routine, including his daily receipt of the Eucharist. Luke is awakened one windy night by Jennifer, his adult daughter. Driving home after a day spent drinking with friends, Jennifer hits a man with her car. Luke drives to the scene and discovers the man's body. Here Dubus slows the narrative as Luke catalogs his sins. He did not stop for Father Paul, a priest friend, who might have given the man his last rites; he did not call an ambulance. He came only to protect his daughter. The following morning, Luke receives the Eucharist as usual, but says nothing to Father Paul about the incident. "It is a world of secrets," he thinks, and "that is the nature of fatherhood."[89] And, he tells the reader, he would "do it again" because his daughter "woke what had flowed dormant in my blood since her birth, so that what rose from the bed was not a stable owner or a Catholic or any other Luke Ripley I had lived with for a long time, but the father of a girl."[90]

Luke would not have protected his sons this way; he would have called the police. Not because he loves them less, but because "I could bear the pain of watching and knowing my son's pain."[91] God could not understand the loss of a daughter, he says; God "could not have borne her passion."[92] Dubus does not replace God with man, but he does reveal how the sharp edges of life can derail even the soundest ethical sensibility. He makes no pretensions toward theology, as Luke's first-person experiences apply only to his own moments, and no others. The sacramental love of Dubus's fiction may be broken and uneven, but that love is dogged.

Dubus once said: "I can't write about a character I can't love."[93] Dubus captured the Catholic worldview that shaped the sufferings and sorrows of his characters. His men and women might behave badly, but they are Catholic to the bone, and the soul. Being a real Catholic might be too hard for Luke Ripley, but Dubus knew something important about that struggle: it makes for great stories.

The most often-told story about Dubus's own life happened on July 23, 1986, on Route 93 in Massachusetts. Coming home from doing research for a story, Dubus stopped to help two stranded motorists whose car had struck an abandoned motorcycle. As another car headed for them, Dubus was able to push one of the motorists out of the way—the other was struck and killed. Dubus was also hit. This selfless act left Dubus paralyzed. As he describes it, "I do not remember leaving the ground my two legs stood on for the last instant in my life, then moving through the air, over the car's hood and windshield and roof, and falling on its trunk."[94]

A writer known for his physicality on and off the page, Dubus sank into despair. His friends and admirers came to the rescue. On a sequence of Sundays in February and March 1987, at the Charles Hotel in Harvard Square, there was a dream reading series: John Irving, Kurt Vonnegut, Ann Beattie, Stephen King, Tim O'Brien, John Updike, Gail Godwin, Richard Yates, Jayne Anne Phillips, and E. L. Doctorow. The readings were followed by dinners: fundraising events for "a little-known writer of short stories who was struck by a car," as described in Associated Press coverage of the event. That little-known writer was Andre Dubus.

The reading series helped put Dubus on the wider literary map, but only relatively so. He remains the quintessential writer's writer, more appreciated than he is widely read. We might blame the omission on the lament that short stories have fewer readers than novels, but equally likely is the literary problem of his sincere Catholicism. While a student in the MFA program at Iowa, Dubus studied with the novelist R. V. Cassill, who once told him: "You're good at writing down what people do, and say, and what they look like. But you don't have the killer instinct of a Catholic novelist to go deeply and find out why they're doing it."[95] Perhaps it is folly to closely parse a literary statement made in a bar, and yet the chosen vocabulary is so enticing. By the time he was regularly publishing short fiction, Dubus certainly had a "Catholic killer storytelling instinct." His talent was clear. His religious sincerity, though, could confound readers.

For a practicing Catholic writer like Dubus, the Eucharist is not *merely* symbol and metaphor; it is symbol, metaphor, and literal body of Christ. Getting an audience to love your story is one thing; getting that audience to take your theology seriously is, perhaps, nothing short of a miracle.

O'Connor and Percy differed from Dubus because his style made his religion transparent: his Catholicism was naked on the page. O'Connor's Catholic faith was made strange by her characters and settings; Percy's Catholic faith was layered in philosophy. "I speak in a Christian context," Percy explained in an essay. "That is to say, I do not conceive it my vocation to preach the Christian faith in a novel, but as it happens, my world view is informed by a certain belief about man's nature and destiny which cannot fail to be central to any novel I write."[96] Percy wondered himself if readers needed to share O'Connor's theological vision in order to appreciate, or even understand, her stories. Perhaps it is O'Connor's mysterious strength that while her theology undergirds her fiction, her stories transcend acceptance of her dogma. Fiction refracts more than it reflects, and the mysterious process of great stories makes us believers in something. Some might call that narrative; others have a different name for it.

O'Connor, Percy, and Dubus were all practicing Catholic fiction writers and by all measures sincere about their faith. They wrote theologically rich fiction. Their stories might sometimes push the orthodox limits of Catholicism, but they were never heretical. God was present in their stories, but presence does not equal lived perfection. They wrote of fallible men and women. As Dubus once said, in the words of a "wise Jesuit" who visited his high school: "If there were no sins, there wouldn't be art."[97]

An apt quote to capture the spirit of Catholic fiction in twentieth-century America, but another might be even better. For years, Dubus tried to publish in *Esquire*, whose fiction editor, Rust Hills, had been so kind to O'Connor. He finally published there in 1996, three years before his death. Years earlier, he shopped "The Pretty Girl" to Hills, who passed on the story, but offered some encouraging words: "God, I like this. Why don't you add forty pages to it. . . . You could make a lot of money. Nobody writes about this Catholic blood and guts."[98]

It was a prescient comment: both accurate and not. In the past few decades, Catholic writers in America have been thriving, but they are Catholic writers of a different vein than Dubus, Percy, and O'Connor. Readers, religious and otherwise, detect the incarnational moments in their fiction, their literal and symbolic blood and guts. But their God is absent.

3

CULTURAL PIETY

Don DeLillo's Catholicism without Belief

"There's no escape from the Jesuits," warned Don DeLillo.[1] He was speaking to students at St. Louis University, a Jesuit college, in 2010. Fifty-two years earlier, he'd graduated from another Jesuit school, Fordham University in the Bronx. Founded in the sixteenth century by Ignatius of Loyola, the Jesuits have been doctors, lawyers, professors, writers, activists, and scholars. Most importantly, they are priests and brothers who make vows of poverty, chastity, and obedience. Their motto is *Ad Majorem Dei Gloriam*—for the greater glory of God.

DeLillo couldn't escape the Jesuits because he'd been trained by them. Ignatian spirituality is defined by the idea that God is present in all things. The Jesuit education that DeLillo received at Fordham was grounded in the belief that the divine was simultaneously among us and beyond us; both tangible and conceptual. A rigorous intellectual education, it was also buoyed by the Ignatian tendency toward reflection, best exemplified by the Examen, a nightly prayer of presence, gratitude, and emotion.

DeLillo also couldn't escape the Jesuits because he grew up in their shadow. He lived in a house on the corner of East 182nd Street and Adams Place, a fifteen-minute walk from Fordham. The next block over from DeLillo's home was Arthur Avenue, the Bronx's center of Italian immigrants like DeLillo's own parents. His literal and liturgical sense of the world was created by Catholicism and his Italian ethnicity. It seems his family emigrated from near Montagano, in southern Italy, around the time of World War I. Southern Italian Catholics are known for the independence of their piety. They are no less devoted than other Catholics, but tend to be focused on the rituals shared by fellow members of the laity: prayer, devotion to the saints, and regional tradition rather than deference to the priesthood and the institutional church.

Born on November 20, 1936, DeLillo inherited the American immigrant family's tension to conform without rejecting old culture and tradition. It is no easy task. DeLillo explains: "What a writer does—a writer from a certain background—is write himself out of his neighborhood and into the broader culture."[2] His neighborhood was Catholic and Italian, and his education was parochial. By his own description, DeLillo received "sixteen years of Catholic education," including grade school, Cardinal Hayes High School, and Fordham.[3]

"For a Catholic," DeLillo reflected in an interview, "nothing is too important to discuss or think about, because he's raised with the idea that he will die any minute now and that if he doesn't live his life in a certain way this death is simply an introduction to an eternity of pain. This removes a hesitation that a writer might otherwise feel when he's approaching important subjects, eternal subjects. I think for a Catholic these things are part of ordinary life."[4] Such a concept—that life is eternal and immediate, that his youthful Bronx world of asphalt and corner store was part of a grand theological order—is distinctly Jesuit.

DeLillo has often spoken of his Catholic formation and childhood, emphasizing that while this education was foundational, it is distinctly in the past. Yet if one can't escape the Jesuits at seventy-three years old, even in jest, how is that possible? The paradox speaks to a unique form of cultural piety created by Jesuit education, a type of piety that is particular to those in the Ignatian tradition, but certainly not exclusive to DeLillo.

The first sentence of DeLillo's first published interview, from 1982, is revelatory. When asked why reference books only give his date of birth and no other personal information, DeLillo responded "Silence, exile, cunning, and so on."[5] Those words are taken from one of the final pages of *A Portrait of the Artist as a Young Man* by James Joyce, a novel about a young man's growth away from the Ireland and the Church of his youth. Stephen Dedalus is speaking about his plans with his friend Cranly. He makes a grand proclamation: "I will not serve that in which I no longer believe, whether it call itself my home, my fatherland, or my church: and I will try to express myself in some mode of life or art as freely as I can and as wholly as I can, using for my defence the only arms I allow myself to use—silence, exile, and cunning."[6] Stephen's defiant words recall Lucifer's *non serviam*, a reference that would be especially enticing to Joyce, who left the church, telling his then-girlfriend Nora Barnacle that he hated "it most fervently" and he made "open war upon it by what I write and say and do."[7]

To leave the church was one thing; to escape the Jesuits was something else entirely. Joyce had attended Clongowes Wood and Belvedere College, both Jesuit-run schools. When his religion had been discussed in a book by critic Frank Budgen, Joyce responded "You allude to me as a Catholic. Now for the sake of precision and to get the correct contour on me, you ought to allude to me as a Jesuit."[8]

These might seem like the sarcastic quibbles of a notoriously wry author. Yet Joyce had a profound respect for the intellectual flexibility and range of the Jesuits, even if he had long ago parted ways with their God. DeLillo's divorce from belief is muddier. He speaks of being Catholic, and being trained by Jesuits, in different ways. On Catholicism, he is nostalgic and ruminating. He says "the ritual had elements of art to it. . . . Sometimes it was awesome; sometimes it was funny. High funeral masses were a little of both, and they're among my warmest childhood memories."[9] We can imagine young DeLillo in the Bronx, somewhere between smirking and sentimental.

In contrast, DeLillo speaks of the Jesuits with a Joycean respect. Speaking of his time at Fordham, he said "the Jesuits taught me to be a failed ascetic."[10] In a conversation with Gerald Howard, his editor at Viking for *Libra* and a fellow New York Catholic, DeLillo seemed as if he was speaking to a classmate. Howard joked "I think your lifelong allegiance to Father Joyce has paid off splendidly," to which DeLillo responded "[Norman] Mailer calls him Doctor Joyce. You and I know that he's a priest."[11]

That lifelong allegiance began with *Ulysses*, Joyce's Modernist tome that seems heretical at a superficial glance—the first page includes a parody of the Eucharist—but is a deeply Jesuit work. DeLillo has summarized his own sensibility, his "sense of humor" and "dark approach to things," as being part New York, part Catholic, and to a lesser extent formed by his reading.[12] Chief among them was Joyce's novel. DeLillo "was very taken by the beauty of the language," perhaps the highest possible compliment from a writer who sees as his true literary purpose the creation of clear and true sentences.[13]

DeLillo directly contrasts Joyce's learned, Jesuit syntaxes with the Italian Catholic culture of his Bronx youth, in which reading was "not part of our tradition. People spoke, and yelled, but there wasn't much reading."[14] At Fordham, DeLillo was taught by priests. There the immigrant folk-piety of his youth met the theological complexity of Jesuit thought. Catholicism is a religion of many rooms, and Fordham's education forced DeLillo to contrast the superstitious, old-world faith of his family with the intellectual faith of Jesuit academia. He would have had to attend compulsory Mass. He graduated in 1958 with a "communication arts" degree—one he derides in interviews—yet he would have had to take eight semesters of theology and philosophy.[15]

Fordham marked the end of DeLillo's formal Jesuit education. It also seems to be the end of his Catholic practice, at least what he will publicly discuss. His respect for the Jesuits, and their clear literary and philosophical influence on him, suggest that he receded from religious practice for other reasons. Soon after graduation, he began working as a copywriter for Ogilvy, Benson and Mather advertising agency, and lived in a small apartment in the Murray Hill section of Manhattan. The May 12, 1960 issue of *The Fordham Ram*, the newspaper of his alma mater, includes the announcement that DeLillo had published his first short story, "The River Jordan," in *Epoch*, the literary magazine of Cornell University. Never reprinted, the story was about Emil Burke, a quirky storefront preacher of the Psychic Church of the Crucified Christ.

DeLillo continued to write while working for the advertising agency. *Esquire* rejected a story of his in 1962, the same year

DeLillo was reaching out to literary agents for representation. He quit his advertising job in 1964, ostensibly to write, but he spent many afternoons at the movie theater. His writing fortunes slowly improved. A positive rejection from *The New Yorker* in 1966 was followed by an acceptance by *The Kenyon Review*, and soon thereafter an appearance in *Carolina Quarterly*, again in *Epoch*, and several appearances in *Sports Illustrated*, including a partial serialization of what would become his second novel, *End Zone*.

We know DeLillo's literary ambitions of these years, but we know nothing of his religious or spiritual practice. He seems to have left his formal adherence to the Catholic Church at the doors of Fordham, and yet even before then, he was careful to note that his Catholic and Jesuit identities often diverged. The superstitious, provincial Catholicism of his Italian family was foreign from the rigorous, intellectual Catholicism of his classroom— although they were united in Christ.

Several months after DeLillo graduated from Fordham, Pope John XXIII delivered a surprise: "We announce to you, indeed trembling a little with emotion, but at the same time with humble resolution of intention, the name and the proposal of a twofold celebration: a diocesan synod for the city, and an ecumenical council for the Universal Church."[16] Pope John XXIII had called for an *aggiornamento*: an opening of the doors of the church, a reconsideration of the relationship between the church and the wider world.

That renewal was Vatican II, which began in 1962 and ended in 1965, concluding with proclamations about liturgy, the role of the church in the modern world, and ecumenical relationships. The traditional Latin rite—the universal language that made for the grand theater of Mass during DeLillo's youth—would be replaced by the local tongue of parish communities. Priests would no longer worship *ad orientem*—"to the east," the traditional practice of celebrating Mass—and would instead face the congregation. What had been a formal, highly ritualized spectacle became more vernacular, common, and everyday. Yet because he had drifted from the church during these intervening years, Latin, and not English, was DeLillo's religious language, and the music of his unbelief.

In 1971, then a full-time writer mostly publishing technical nonfiction, DeLillo released his first novel, *Americana*. The novel begins with a scene of December languor: "Then we came to the end of another dull and lurid year. Lights were strung across the front of every shop. Men selling chestnuts wheeled their smoky carts."[17] The city street is full of bell-ringing Santas and Salvation Army bands: "It was a strange sound to hear in that time and place, the smack of cymbals and high-collared drums, a suggestion that children were being scolded for a bottomless sin, and it seemed to annoy people."[18] The book's first page is gently disorienting, as if we are waking from a dream. It is a proper opening for a writer whose prose is often so precise that we feel as if he's put us in a trance.

DeLillo's debut is the story of David Bell, a quirky and ambitious television executive. It is also, aptly, the story of America—first through the city. The early description of an urban crowd is prototypical DeLillo: "Below Forty-Second Street, people were able to choose their own pace and yet here the faces seemed gray and stricken, the bodies surreptitious in the scrawls of their coats, and it occurred to me that perhaps in this city the crowd was essential to the individual; without it, he had nothing against which to scrape his anger, no echo for grief, and not the slightest proof that there were others more lonely than he."[19]

Americana is the introduction to themes that have made DeLillo a laureate for his age: the individual in contrast with the crowd, paranoia, and a darkly spiritual vision in which the most mundane moments and places are imbued with an otherworldly hue. In one scene, Bell describes his father's collection of TV commercials that he stores in the basement: "I thought of him standing by the projector as the first new reel of the evening thrust its image through the dust-drizzling church-light toward the screen."[20] In the most mundane of spaces, a family's basement, the prosaic is transmogrified into something magical.

Bell was raised Episcopalian in Old Holly, a fictional suburb of New York City. In *Americana* and other novels—including *End Zone* and the pseudonymously written farce *Amazons*—DeLillo seems to enjoy writing about small country towns. If we consider DeLillo's desire to "write himself out of his neighborhood and into the broader culture," for an Italian kid from the Bronx, the mythic America is not Arthur Avenue; it is Norman Rockwell and farm-lands .[21]

When DeLillo writes of the city, he often does so with a smirk. Yet he is earnest when describing small-town America. Homes in the town are old, "agreeably shabby."[22] We hear "no more than intimations from the keys of a lidded piano, no more than cutlery and voices, the indolent sermon of a saw on wood, no more than silence or the stagnant inner sound which silence contains in all old rooms deep in sunlight."[23] Beautiful, lyric lines that suggest a certain longing from the character—and the writer.

Bell attended services at the Episcopal church with his mother, a "genuinely devout" woman who "was uneasy about the whole idea of the passion of Christ."[24] DeLillo writes Protestants as a Catholic would, based on assumption and stereotype: her Christianity is proper, formal, and clean. Her vision of Jesus "was a blond energetic lad who had helped his mother around the house and occasionally performed a nifty miracle."[25]

A typical summer Sunday in Old Holly meant the whole town congregated at places of worship, "neat white churches" that stand "in groves of sunlight."[26] *Americana* has the feel of a skilled writer's early novel—certain stretches move toward wordplay and away from plot—but DeLillo demonstrates his storytelling method in a simple scene:

> Grandfather cops, absurd gunbelts over their paunches, direct whatever traffic is coming out of the church parking lots after services. The worshippers come down the steps blinking and damp, moving slowly and with the extreme caution which a new and vaster environment always exacts, heading across lawns or toward the parking lots where their cars seem to be swimming in the bluesteel incandescence of the gravel. Metal hot to the touch and hell-stench inside. On Sundays, in the wide rows of light, it's as though all the torpor of Christianity itself is spread over the land.[27]

DeLillo's descriptive power comes from his control over syntax. His clauses, full of rich and often surprising detail, lean against commas. His punctuation lifts sentences, as if they are spoken with a grand cadence. Faith sends mystical shivers through the town, bending reality in a slight but tangible way.

This is not to suggest Bell is pious. He is sarcastic, sardonic, rough, and ironic. He is a unique creation, a Protestant character brewed by a Jesuit mind, and *Americana* is best understood as a wild character sketch of him. Bell attended St. Dymphna (patron saint of mental illness and epilepsy), an Episcopal private school in New Hampshire. Bell is intrigued with Brad Dennis—a Catholic on the basketball team, infamous around campus for making the sign of the cross before taking foul shots—a fitting bullhorn for DeLillo. Brad's mom said "St. Dymphna was an exclusively Catholic saint and that the Episcopalians, as nice and neat as they were, had no claim to her patronage and absolutely no right to use her name in connection with one of their prep schools."[28] Brad "distributed literature published by the Knights of Columbus, and he offered to debate anyone his age on the relative merits of the world's great religions. Some of us would meet illegally in his room after lights-out to hear him discourse on the transubstantiation and papal infallibility."[29]

This is Jesuit humor; think DeLillo at Fordham, sitting in courses titled "The Quadriform Gospel" and "Alpha and Omega," daydreaming of theological jokes.[30] Brad evolves from handing out leaflets for the Franciscan Missions to skepticism of "that kid stuff about virgin saints. . . . The modern Catholic is a hard-nosed kind of guy who asks piercing questions. The whole thing can be brought down to a question of metaphysics and first principles."[31]

Bell is fascinated by Brad's stories and flexible theology. Years later, Bell's father also feels the pull of the church and admits that he's thinking about converting. His father has become friends with a priest, who "told me all about the human soul. The soul has a transcendental connection to the body. It informs the body. The soul becomes aware of its own essence after it separates from the body. Once you're dead, your soul can be directly illuminated by God."[32]

It sounds like his father has been talking to a Jesuit, who would continually stress the interplay of mind, body, and spirit (soul). Bell understands his father's desire for something more. Bell feels that he and his father are not the only ones who long for God and meaning: "All the bright young men of Madison Avenue searched for some facsimile of danger, some black root which might crack the foundation of their basic Episcopalianism, and we looked to the milder psychedelics, the study of karate, the weekend skydiving club, the sports-car rally."[33] Disillusioned and bored with his television network job, Bell goes on a road trip, a pilgrimage, with his friend Sullivan. Other companions join them along the way, and they have esoteric conversations that feel as if they came out of Jesuit philosophy and conjecture: "Sullivan filled the moody silence by announcing that my digression on numbers was somewhat less than Euclidean in its sweep and purity; that one of my main faults was a tendency to get blinded by the neon of an idea, never reaching truly inside it; that to follow a number to infinity was not necessarily to arrive at God."[34]

Among these conversations bordering on ecclesiastical and obscure, DeLillo returns to his mundane settings. Bell and his friends "wandered through the kitchen and pantry, feeling I had come to the heart of something, to the secret of the terror of small towns on Sunday, the Eucharistic silence of coffee and buns after the long walk back from church."[35] Somehow this lapsed Episcopalian first-person narrator uses Catholic language and cadence to describe his trip: "What a mysterious and sacramental journey, I thought."[36] The language becomes more spiritual the further he progresses, as if Bell is gaining God by proxy: "I am falling silently through myself. The spirit contracts at the termination of every passion."[37]

In the novel's final scene, Bell has crisscrossed down to Texas, on the most American of pilgrimages: Dealey Plaza. He slams his hand on the car horn and holds it there as he drives past the School Book Depository and "beneath the triple underpass."[38] He uses his American Express credit card to buy a ticket to New York, and the novel ends on his flight—the wayfaring man taken up to the heavens.

DeLillo said *Americana* took him years to write for two reasons: "I had to keep interrupting it to earn a living," and "I didn't know what I was doing."[39] The novel's meandering route feels appropriate for Bell's wavering journey, yet DeLillo was aware of its "structural problems."[40] His own judgement might be too harsh, but DeLillo needed another novel to even out his debut. A few weeks after finishing *Americana*, he began writing *End Zone*, which took "about one-fourth the time" it did to write his first book.[41]

Punchy, risky, sarcastic yet focused, *End Zone* is DeLillo's first accomplished book, a novel about theology, football, college, language, and race. The first eight chapters of the novel originally appeared in *Sports Illustrated*, and by that time, DeLillo had stopped his advertising and technical work and only wrote fiction. *End Zone* is saturated with Jesuit touches: the football players living an existence full of exile and cunning in the desert; the study of linguistics as a way to unearth metaphysical secrets; the football coach as grandfather who descends into a sick shell, a man who becomes all soul and spirit by novel's end.

As was previously noted, early in the novel, the narrator, Gary Harkness, reflects on a past coach who joked "People don't go to football games to see pass patterns run by theologians."[42] Gary's inclinations and obsessions are patently Jesuit, but not quite Catholic in a devotional sense. He is more of a curious seeker than a genuine believer. His Protestant coach exhorts the team to pray, but Gary is not attracted to belief; he is interested in the linguistic element of liturgy. He is drawn to the ascetic trappings of intense devotion.

Gary is a Christian without Christ—an absurd paradox, but one that feels appropriate to DeLillo, a secular Jesuit who is a cultural Catholic. Much like Joyce's character of Stephen Dedalus, Gary loves exile, on a campus out in the quiet, desolate west Texas desert. "Simplicity, repetition, solitude, starkness, discipline upon discipline"—those are his rhythms.[43] Logos College is "in the middle of the middle of nowhere," among "terrain so flat and bare, suggestive of the end of recorded time, a splendid sense of remoteness firing my soul."[44]

Gary's obsessions are bizarre. He is drawn to war and finds dark pleasure in the language of annihilation. He envisions war as a game, but stops short of actually participating. He does not join the ROTC programs on campus, but instead audits courses that allow him to fall into the rhythms of military language without causing harm. The only violence Gary craves is the controlled violence of the football field, and once the season ends, he is lost. He wanders campus. He stops eating. His ascetic tendencies become hallucinations, and yet in those pathological states, he becomes more spirit than body.

Catholic Mass isn't football, but they share the concept of ritual: learned, practiced movements whose repetition instills a heightened sense. A logos of locomotion. "People whose lives are not clearly shaped or marked off may feel a deep need for rules of some kind," DeLillo has said.[45] They might seek religion; they might also embrace games. "Most games are carefully structured," DeLillo explained.[46] "They satisfy a sense of order and they even have an element of dignity about them."[47]

These games "provide a frame in which we try to be perfect," a phrase with biblical construction.[48] DeLillo's characters are not perfect in Christ; they are haunted by a distant God, and seem to waste away as the novel goes on. The players participate in "an extremely simple-minded game" around campus, in which they make the shape of a gun and mimic the sound of a killing shot.[49] What starts as an immature joke evolves into a strangely poetic performance; "it forced cracks into the enveloping silence."[50] The game "enabled us to pretend that death could be a tender experience," filling a spiritual void for the players.[51] At the same time,

Gary's roommate, a 300-pound player named Anatole Bloomberg, is on a quest to "unjew"[52] himself; to erase his Jewish identity, to break from the "guilt of being innocent victims."[53]

Late in the novel, longing for the now distant season, Gary becomes a secular monk. He begins having long ruminations on silence: "Everywhere it was possible to perceive varieties of silence . . . small pauses in corners, rectangular planes of stillness, the insides of desks and closets (where shoes curl in dust), the spaces between things, the endless silence of surfaces, time swallowed by methodically silent clocks."[54] Gary does not quite find peace at the conclusion of *End Zone*, but he does become dissociated from his body. He occupies an elemental state. We might call his soul perfected, in a way. Gary believes in language more than he believes in Christ. His bizarre theological vision—a desire to find eternal meaning in football through his self-imposed exile—can only exist as a monastic dream.

End Zone suggests that DeLillo's youthful experiences with language—a Latin he couldn't fully understand, but could speak, recite, sing—enabled him to find spiritual rhythms in syntax. Catholic Mass, especially the Latin Mass of DeLillo's faithful years, is a spectacle of song, repeated physical movements and gestures, stories, and smells. The narrative of such a Mass lies within the power of its weekly, rhythmic refrain rather than the often unknown content of its language.

Great Jones Street, his next novel, begins with a spiritual testament from Bucky Wunderlick, an exasperated rock star. "Toward the end of the final tour," he laments, "it became apparent that our audience wanted more than music, more even than its own reduplicated noise."[55] He stood among them, "in the incandescent pit of a huge stadium filled with wildly rippling bodies, all totally silent."[56] Bucky is a mystic. He channels the ineffable.

Exhausted from the excesses of fame, Bucky flies home to New York City. He retreats into a "small crooked room" to escape the world.[57] In *End Zone*, Gary Harkness exiled himself to the desert; in *Great Jones Street*, Bucky "became a half-saint, practiced in visions" inside a small room in a big city.[58] Visitors interrupt his solitude. Fans, managers, bandmates: everyone wants him to reemerge. "Your power is growing," they tell him, "the more time you spend in isolation, the more demands are made on the various media to communicate some relevant words and pictures."[59] At the end of the book, Bucky emerges from a drug-induced haze to learn the rumors about his new life are legion. In one, he is "living among beggars and syphilitics, performing good works, patron saint of all those men who hear the river-whistles sing the mysteries and who return to sleep in wine by the south wheel of the city."[60]

Zero K, DeLillo's latest novel, arrives at similar themes of secular mysticism, but is perhaps his darkest book. Billionaire Ross Lockhart is funding a mysterious project that includes cryonic suspension: the preservation of bodies until the future, when medical advances might offer extended life. Ross says "everybody wants to own the end of the world," but it soon becomes clear that for a powerful man like Ross, the end of the self is the end of the universe.[61] Artis, his second wife, is terminally ill. His project is ultimately for her, to save her fragile existence.

Ross's project is called The Convergence. The term "convergence" calls to mind the Jesuit paleontologist Pierre Teilhard de Chardin, whose concept of the Omega Point posits that the universe is evolving toward an ultimate convergence of systems, a perfect consciousness. Flannery O'Connor read and praised Teilhard's work, titling one of her stories "Everything that Rises Must Converge." DeLillo has also read and studied

Teilhard—likely hearing of the Jesuit's provocative theories during his days at Fordham—and said he was compelled by "the idea that human consciousness is reaching a point of exhaustion, and that what comes next may be either a paroxysm or something enormously sublime."[62] That description perfectly captures the final scene of *End Zone*, when Gary Harkness takes his ascetic aspirations to their logical conclusion and stops eating, his dehydrated body wheeled to the campus infirmary. DeLillo even used an inversion of Teilhard's term—it retains the same meaning—as the title of another novel, *Point Omega*.

Zero K might be DeLillo's most agnostic novel, a work that takes Teilhard's superstructure and strips it of God and Christ and other signifiers. If anyone portends to be God in *Zero K*, it is Ross, or the mysterious Stenmark Twins, whose philosophies about war, death, and the afterlife put flesh on the skeleton of the Convergence.

If Ross needs men like the Stenmark Twins to offer a narrative to his cryonic project, he needs his son to bear witness. Jeff, Ross's son, soon realizes that his father wants him to be there when Artis dies. It is a strange tinge of vulnerability for a man who left Jeff and his mother, Madeline, when Jeff was thirteen: "I was doing my trigonometry homework when he told me."[63] Jeff has never quite forgiven his father, but is able to keep both Madeline and Artis in high esteem.

The desert research facility is full of screens that lower from the ceiling and play silent images of destruction and suffering. There Artis seems unafraid of her unknown future, and that unsettles Jeff. An archeologist, she thinks of finding her own self at her cryonic reawakening. Artis, in a true way, needs the Convergence to give her a second chance. Others opt for Zero K, a "special unit" of the facility that is "predicated on the subject's willingness to make a certain kind of transition to the next level."[64]

As Jeff describes it, the Convergence facility exists outside of time, "time compressed, time drawn tight, overlapping time, dayless, nightless, many doors, no windows."[65] The setting recalls the "dense environmental texture" of the supermarket in *White Noise*, where "automatic doors opened and closed, breathing abruptly. Colors and odors seemed sharper."[66] In that space, the sound of gliding feet, newsprint rustle, whispers, and cars rattling over manhole covers created a surreal moment. In *Zero K*, the surreal confluence of screens, strange artwork, empty rooms, long hallways, and shaved heads makes for DeLillo's ultimate ascetic experiment.

DeLillo has said his Catholic youth permeates his work, but in "ways I can't be specific about—the sense of ceremony, the sense of last things, and the sense of religion as almost at times an art."[67] His creed is Catholicism without belief; structure and language without devotion. Faith and doubt are not merely linked in culture and story; they sustain each other. DeLillo's fiction suggests the litanies and liturgies of a writer's youth are not easily discarded. Unbelief itself—clothed in the nostalgia of faith—is a source of spiritual comfort. In fact, for him and other lapsed Catholic writers, God is a source of frustration, fascination, and abject longing.

4

GOD IN THE MACHINE

Thomas Pynchon

A hand reaches from behind the door in a dark apartment, making the peace sign. The arm belongs to a man hiding inside—a man who always seems to be hiding, even when he is in plain sight. It is 1965, in Manhattan Beach, California. The writer Phyllis Gebauer is standing outside the door on a stoop. She is laughing, her eyes hidden behind sunglasses. A pink and white pig piñata named Claude hangs over the railing. The man in the darkness is Thomas Pynchon.

The metaphor seems too perfect. Not even J.D. Salinger, who published a single novel in 1951 and two story collections before leaving public view, has captured the obsession of readers as much as the mythos of Thomas Pynchon. Born in 1937 in Glen Cove, New York, a section of Long Island, Pynchon's family moved to Oyster Bay, where he attended high school and graduated as salutatorian in 1953, at 16 years old. From there he went upstate to Cornell to study engineering, where a friend named Jules Siegel said Pynchon "went to Mass and confessed, though to what would be a mystery."[1] Pynchon's father came from a long line of New England Protestants, who arrived in Massachusetts from England in 1630. He got his Catholicism—the faith he was raised in—from his Irish mother. C. Michael Curtis, longtime fiction editor for *The Atlantic*, roomed with Pynchon and the writer and singer Richard Fariña at Cornell. Curtis described Pynchon as "very Catholic."[2]

Pynchon did well at Cornell, but was a "very private person."[3] After a year of engineering, he began to study English—he had written for his high school newspaper—but left the university during his sophomore year to join the navy. He spent two years in the military, among them some time on the USS *Hank*, a navy destroyer ship in the Mediterranean. *Slow Learner*, Pynchon's lone story collection, contains his longest consideration of the writing life, including some insights into these early days. While on break from shore patrol duty near the navy base in Norfolk, Virginia, Pynchon found an issue of *Evergreen Review* in a bookstore, and was quickly inspired. The magazine had just begun publishing, but early issues included work by Samuel Beckett, Jean-Paul Sartre, Vladimir Nabokov, and Henry Miller. Once back at Cornell in 1957, Pynchon began writing in earnest.

Slow Learner is comprised of those early stories as well as a few written after he graduated in 1959. Although given the chance to teach writing at the university, Pynchon instead moved to Greenwich Village, and began writing what would become his first novel, *V*. That next year, he moved to Seattle to work for Boeing as a technical writer, drafting articles for *BOMARC Service News* while he was writing his creative work—a parallel path as Don DeLillo at the start of his career. Like DeLillo, Pynchon stopped his technical writing when his first novel was published.

V., released in 1963, was not Pynchon's first moment of literary success. His early stories appeared in prestigious publications like *Epoch* and the *Kenyon Review*, and were reprinted in *The Best American Short Stories* and *The O. Henry Prize*. Yet the novel is his first sustained, dizzying entry into a canon of writing as arresting as it is odd.

The novel begins on Christmas Eve, 1955, in Norfolk, Virginia. Benny Profane, recently discharged from the navy, is walking down a bustling street. Profane drinks and parties his way through the new year and meets Paola Maijstral, a Maltese woman who works at the Sailor's Grave, a Norfolk bar. Paola wears a Miraculous Medal around her neck, leading the chapter's narrator to wonder: "What sort of Catholic was she? Profane, who was only half Catholic (mother Jewish) and whose morality was fragmentary (being derived from experience and not much of it), wondered what quaint Jesuit arguments had led her to come away with him, refuse to share a bed, but still ask him to 'be good.'"[4] Profane's father is later described as "devoutly R.C."[5]

Much like DeLillo, Pynchon detaches the Jesuit strand of Catholicism from the larger Catholic religion and worldview. The Catholic characters in *V.* are pious, nostalgic, and superstitious. The Jesuit element is intellectual and rhetorical; to borrow from James Joyce, to be a Jesuit means to be aware of both art and artifice. The Long Island Irish-Catholicism of Pynchon was not incompatible with the literary irreverence he showed as a writer in high school and college. Yet as he grew older, served in the military, and likely became more distant and nostalgic about his childhood, it is conceivable that a born satirist like Pynchon would retain the more faithful elements of Catholicism for his characters, and appropriate the more scholarly elements for himself as author. Pynchon as playful Jesuit seems particularly apt:

the architecture of his novels, and even his sentences, are sweeping and syntactically winding.

V.—appropriate to the shape of the title's letter—splits and never quite converges. Profane's misadventures are interspersed with chapters that tell the story of Herbert Stencil, a man obsessed with finding the secrets of the titular V. The chapters allow young Pynchon ample room for conspiratorial rambling, as Stencil will follow history down any hole to find V., who seems to be a woman, but who also might be a concept.

Early in the novel, it appears that V. might be Victoria Wren, a Catholic girl who attended convent school and "talked perhaps overmuch about her religion; had indeed for a time considered the Son of God as a young lady will consider any eligible bachelor."[6] Even so, she "left the novitiate after a matter of weeks but not the Church: that with its sadfaced statuary, odors of candles and incense, formed along with an uncle Evelyn the foci of her serene orbit."[7] Taken to daydreams, Victoria would spend Mass imagining that "God wore a wide-awake hat and fought skirmishes with an aboriginal Satan out at the antipodes of the firmament, in the name and for the safekeeping of any Victoria."[8]

Stencil's search remains unresolved as the novel returns to Benny Profane, who has his own conquest: a job chasing alligators in the sewers of New York City. Profane's routes lead him down dark corridors and to strange discoveries. He notices the alligators moving uptown into a region known as Fairing's Parish, named after a Jesuit priest. Father Fairing had ministered during the Great Depression at "breadlines and missions, where he gave comfort, stitched up raggedy souls," but worried that the city would be full of "starved corpses."[9] He "decided that the rats were going to take over after New York died."[10]

Father Fairing hatched the only plan he thought possible: he decided to convert the rats to Catholicism. He descended into the sewers with the *Baltimore Catechism* and breviary, and "put an eternal blessing and a few exorcisms on all the water flowing through the sewers between Lexington and the East River and between eighty-sixth and seventy-ninth streets."[11]

Fairing eats rats for sustenance, but also catalogues his attempts at communicating with them. He names a rat Ignatius after the famed Jesuit. He attempts to instruct them on the catechism and has theological debates with them about the early church fathers. One rat named Veronica had a "soul worth saving."[12] She wants to become a nun, but the priest "explained to her that to date there is no recognized order for which she would be eligible."[13] Profane learns these oddball stories and thinks they are apocryphal, but while in the sewers himself, he observes that, in addition to a crucifix, "scrawled on the walls were occasional quotes from the Gospels, Latin tags."[14] Pynchon includes the Roman Rite of his Mass-going years: "Agnus Dei, qui tollis peccata mundi, dona nobis pacem—Lamb of God, who taketh away the sins of the world, grant us peace."[15]

Exhausted and dizzy from chasing alligators, Profane contemplates the strange priest: "Excommunicated, most likely, by the very fact of his mission here, a skeleton in Rome's closet and in the priest-hole of his own cassock and bed, the old man sat preaching to a congregation of rats with saints' names, all to the intention of peace."[16] Profane then finds "a wide space like the nave of a church, an arched roof overhead, a phosphorescent light coming off walls whose exact arrangement was indistinct."[17] The alligator turns to face him: "He waited. He was waiting for something to happen. Something otherworldly, of course. He was sentimental and superstitious."[18] He says sorry as he shoots and kills the alligator.

The Fairing sequence is an appropriate introduction to Pynchon as a Catholic jester and satirist. We know nothing of Pynchon's personal faith after his years at Cornell. Both DeLillo and Pynchon were attending college and going to Mass in New York during the same years, but their spiritual lives afterward are a mystery. DeLillo at least offers us cryptic references in interviews, but we can only mine the reclusive Pynchon's work for clues, and his parodic tone and labyrinthine syntax offer tempting searches. Pynchon's fiction suggests that postmodern writers raised in the Catholic tradition do not merely dispose of the faith once lapsed. In fact, these writers, who were preternaturally drawn toward both high and low culture, symbol and extravagant metaphor, wordplay and literary performance, found all of these elements in a faith they once practiced.

V. is exactly that—a search—whose absurdities only multiply as the pages progress. When a writer's faith lapses, the space occupied by that faith does not simply disappear. Catholicism is an architectural faith—literally, in the grandness of its physical spaces, and theologically. If Pynchon appears to have left the practice of his religion—a conjecture, admittedly, about the most-conjectured about author in contemporary American literature—his religion does not appear to have left his work.

The parodist needs a subject, and Pynchon's subject seems to be our determined, frenetic search for meaning in a world saturated with noise. A young veteran who left heavily manned warships to write about heavily manned aeronautics, Pynchon knew our worst inclinations would only find more potent expression as the years passed. His satirical work is drenched in gloom, and we wonder: Are the jokes themselves the meaning?

The power and song of Pynchon's prose are often lost in his appealing puzzles. In a scene from *V.*, Pynchon includes his fabricated Feast of San' Ercole dei Rinoceronti: the Feast of Saint Hercules of the Rhinoceroses. Pynchon describes Little Italy: "High over all Mulberry Street that night soared arches of light bulbs, arranged in receding sets of whorls, each spanning the street, shining clear to the horizon because the air was so windless."[19] His syntax swirls, but follows a careful route. His descriptions are crisp and new. He is fully capable of being sincere.

Some of the sincerest and most pointed moments of *V.* are the various narrators' pontifications on lost faith. When Victoria Wren returns in a later chapter, we read "her entire commitment to Roman Catholicism as needful and plausible stemmed from and depended on an article of the primitive faith which glimmered shiny and supreme in that reservoir like a crucial valve-handle."[20] The "article" described is Wren's acceptance of the Trinitarian mystery and belief. Paola's father, Fausto, "did nothing so complex as drift away from God or reject his church. Losing faith is a complicated business and takes time. There are no epiphanies, no 'moments of truth'"—only a natural response to the devastation of World War II.[21]

In his attempt to make sense of the madness of his search, Herbert Stencil offers a partial theory: "Truthfully he didn't know what sex V. might be, nor even what genus and species. To go along assuming that Victoria the girl tourist and Veronica the sewer rat were one and the same V. was not at all to bring up any metempsychosis: only to affirm that his quarry fitted in with The Big One, the century's master cabal . . . though V. might be no more a she than a sailing vessel or a nation."[22]

The mysteries of *V.* are never solved, in part because the goal of the search is not linear but experiential. Most critics didn't even try to delineate the book's careening plot, but they could recognize a talented new voice. When *V.* was published, Pynchon was living in Mexico City. In a letter to his agent, Candida Donadio, Pynchon describes two *Time* magazine reporters who showed up at his door, causing him to flee out the back window. While in Mexico City, Pynchon claimed that he was writing four novels at once, and by the next year, he was working on a "potboiler" that is a "short story, but with gland trouble"—and hopes Donadio "can unload it on some poor sucker."[23] That book is *The Crying of Lot 49*.

"The World (This One), the Flesh (Mrs. Oedipa Maas), and the Testament of Pierce Inverarity" appeared in the December 1, 1965 issue of *Esquire*. Although the excerpt is the first chapter of *The Crying of Lot 49*, the true origin of the book is the story "Entropy" from the Spring 1960 issue of *The Kenyon Review*. Meatball Mulligan's lease-breaking party is in its second full day. Benzedrine and champagne are fueling a ruckus on the kitchen floor. A quartet of musicians "wore hornrimmed sunglasses and rapt expressions" as they crouched "over a 15-inch speaker which had been bolted into the top of a wastepaper basket."[24] Several women who worked for intelligence agencies, including the NSA, "had passed out on couches, chairs and in one case the bathroom sink."[25] Meatball himself begins the story inert, "holding an empty [champagne] magnum to his chest as if it were teddy bear."[26]

Pynchon's plot doesn't so much develop as it vibrates. The party rustles Meatball's upstairs neighbor, Callisto, "from an uneasy sleep."[27] "Hermetically sealed," his room "was a tiny enclave of regularity in the city's chaos, alien to the vagaries of the weather, of national politics, of any civil disorder."[28] Callisto ponders entropy—the theoretical heat-death of the universe— while a woman named Aubade shares the tenuous space with him. Callisto had been cradling a small bird for the past three days in an attempt to warm it back to health; he theorized that since heat could not disappear, he could transfer his body heat to help the bird recover. His plan fails, and Aubade, tired of being cooped up, "tore away the drapes and smashed out the glass with two exquisite hands which came away bleeding and glistening with splinters."[29]

Pynchon ends the story with a darkly melodic pronouncement, as the "hovering, curious dominant of their separate lives should resolve into a tonic of darkness and the final absence of all motion."[30] "Entropy" is the story of what happens when a closed system—a social and spiritual experiment—is broken. It is a story without profluence; a story, as Pynchon described in the collection's introduction, that began "with a theme, symbol or other abstract unifying agent" rather than character.[31] Writing nearly twenty-five years since the story's original publication, Pynchon is hard on his younger self, claiming his characters are "synthetic, insufficiently alive," and that he'd gotten "too conceptual, too cute and remote."[32] Yet for all of its self-perceived failures, "Entropy" is the story that Pynchon writes about the most in his introduction to *Slow Learner*, which means it is the one work that he publicly discusses the most. Even if the story was imperfect, the central concept stayed with him: "Since I wrote this story I have kept trying to understand entropy, but my grasp becomes less sure the more I read."[33] Entropy becomes a convenient metaphor for Pynchon; a secularization of a theology. "Entropy" feels like the sketch of an idea that needed a plot; Pynchon only needed to look at the world around him.

The Crying of Lot 49 was published a year after the first chapter was excerpted in *Esquire*. To understand the culture that received Pynchon's book, we have to understand the context—one that had a distinctly Catholic hue. Pynchon's Catholic winks in the *Esquire* title are merely a hint; in the sixties, he, like so many others, was reading the theories of Canadian philosopher and media theorist

Marshall McLuhan. In a 1968 letter to a graduate student named Thomas F. Hirsch, Pynchon confirms his interest in McLuhan's books and ideas. *The Crying of Lot 49*, both temporally and philosophically, resides nicely among McLuhan's seminal works of the decade: *The Gutenberg Galaxy* (1962), *Understanding Media* (1964), and *The Medium Is the Massage* (1967).

A particular Catholic intellectual and artistic renaissance was happening in the mid-1960s—one that existed on a different strand than the fiction of Flannery O'Connor, Walker Percy, J. F. Powers, and other more narratively traditional writers. In 1967, McLuhan's *The Medium Is the Massage* was an eccentric journey into how our senses experience electric media. That same year, Walter Ong, SJ—whose graduate thesis adviser happened to be McLuhan—released *The Presence of the Word*, a dense but visionary take on our evolution from oral to electronic communication. Also in 1967 Andy Warhol created an iconic silkscreen portfolio of Marilyn Monroe. "The more you look at the same exact thing," Warhol said, "the more the meaning goes away, and the better and emptier you feel."[34]

McLuhan, Ong, and Warhol offered a profound vision of media—a Catholic vision. Their Catholicism was not incidental to their theories and their art; it was their structure, their spirit and their sustenance. Their synthesis of tradition and postmodernism offers a fresh way to look at Pynchon's playfulness and style, and suggests that there is something endemic to Catholicism that fueled Pynchon's vision.

"I make probes," wrote Marshall McLuhan. "I don't explain—I explore"; words that sound much like Pynchon's method.[35] Pynchon's playful fictions offer questions, journeys, and possibilities rather than answers. All oracles must divine from somewhere, and McLuhan's source was the Jesuit priest

Pierre Teilhard de Chardin, a touchstone of DeLillo. Teilhard had conceived of the "noösphere," an evolutionary phase in which a "thinking skin" covers the world. This "stupendous thinking machine" of a collective consciousness sounds much like a biological internet.[36] Teilhard's wild theory appealed to an academic like McLuhan, a literary scholar seeking patterns and connections in the history of media and communication.

McLuhan had written the former *America* magazine editor Clement McNaspy, SJ, of his intellectual plan: "We must confront the secular in its most confident manifestations, and, with its own terms and postulates, to shock it into awareness of its confusion, its illiteracy, and the terrifying drift of its logic. There is no need to mention Christianity. It is enough that it be known that the operator is a Christian."[37]

Even that, it seems, was trouble. Although McLuhan's conception of the "global village" created from technology was clearly indebted to Teilhard's noösphere—consider lines like "the evolutionary process has shifted from biology to technology in an eminent degree since electricity"[38] from a letter to philosopher Jacques Maritain, implying an organic sense to electronic media—he shied from acknowledging the French Jesuit's work. In his book *Hooking Up*, the writer Tom Wolfe offers two reasons for this. As a Catholic convert, McLuhan was "highly devout," and "the Church had declared Teilhard's work heterodox."[39] And despite McLuhan's private aspirations in his letters, he was a member of the secular intellectual community and had to avoid overt religious references.

McLuhan's *The Medium Is the Massage* is the work of a theorist at play. The book contains mini-essays, prose poems, and typographic puzzles, juxtaposed with complementary and contrasting images, photographs, drawings, clippings from media and excerpts from James Joyce (the book was a collaboration with graphic designer Quentin Fiore). Ranging from the bizarre to the baroque, McLuhan's collection of objects and texts are exactly on Pynchon's wavelength. Pop culture literally pops into Pynchon's stories as both plot and parody, suggesting a simultaneous tendency to examine and be obsessed with such material. Pynchon's literary worlds dramatize the evolving media landscape that McLuhan sought to document. Although McLuhan's particular focus was on television, he was clear that "all media work us over completely."[40] Hence the *massage*: We are rubbed and relaxed by media. We enter another state.

In the electric river of television, "information pours upon us, instantaneously and continuously."[41] As a viewer, "images are projected at you. You are the screen. The images wrap around you. You are the vanishing point."[42] If "electric technology fosters and encourages unification and involvement," it also disallows escape.[43] The digital world is not going anywhere, and neither are we.

Those prayers, probes, pleas—whatever you would like to call them—are best understood through his context as a Catholic. That identity slowly became more obvious as McLuhan responded to both praise and critiques of his work. After quipping, "I have been bitterly reproached by my Catholic confrères for my lack of scholastic terminology and concepts," he proceeded to offer a firm public stance: "The Christian concept of the mystical body—all men as members of the body of Christ—this becomes technologically a fact under electronic conditions."[44] McLuhan realized that the suffusion of electronic media in the world had a symbolism that was almost transubstantial: Christ everywhere. McLuhan's Catholicism compelled him to seek synthesis and pattern; a world connected through electronics could be seen as having a digital flesh.

McLuhan's ideas are often porous and therefore often misunderstood. He was a disruptor. Yet his ultimate goal was not the "opaquities and obliquities" of value judgments, but rather he was "interested in understanding processes."[45] McLuhan was inspirational, and that can be clearly seen in the work of his former student, Walter Ong, whose insights in *The Presence of the Word* capture an information age that Pynchon would dramatize in fiction.

Early in the book Ong introduces an analogy: "It is useful to think of cultures in terms of the organization of the sensorium . . . the entire sensory apparatus as an operational complex."[46] We are overwhelmed with noise, and culture teaches us how to specialize, how to organize our perception.

The digital world that Ong observed during the mid-'60s was simultaneous, absolute, overwhelming in possibility. Electronic media had projected humanity "across the globe, creating an intensity of self-possession on the part of the human race which is a new, and at times an upsetting, experience. Further transmutations lie ahead."[47] Ong questions the spiritual state of a world redefined by electronics: "Could the cry of Nietzsche's madman, 'God is dead', derive from the fact that He cannot be readily found by the old signs in the newly organized sensorium where the word stands in such different relationship to the total complex of awareness by which man earlier situated himself in his life world?"[48] Our search for God in a newly digital world must be undertaken with new methods. God's absence, then, might be more a question of our inability to discern his presence.

In his 1982 book *Orality and Literacy*, Ong situates Pynchon's literary style along the same continuum of absence and presence. Ong claims that Pynchon's fiction is full of "bizarrely hollowed characters that represent extreme states of consciousness . . . [which] achieve their effects because of the contrast felt with their antecedents, the 'round' characters of the classical novel."[49] Ong might have taken this a step further: Pynchon's tendency toward parody, coupled with his Catholic formation, creates a tension between tradition and satire: the latter is impossible without the former.

While McLuhan and Ong were contemplating the future, another Catholic was living it. In 1967 Andy Warhol was staging his multimedia "Exploding Plastic Inevitable" events across the country. Strobe lights pulsed. Projectors reeled Warhol's films against the walls. Dancers and their shadows cut through the images. Loudspeakers boomed simultaneous pop songs. The Velvet Underground, the band Warhol managed and produced in his own Warholian way, played live.

Nobody would label the content of Warhol's provocative shows as Catholic, but that would be mistaking the media for the message. Warhol's shows were sensory manipulations and experiences. He wanted to alter their states. McLuhan appreciated Warhol's experiments enough to include a collage spread from the show in *The Medium Is the Massage*. Black-and-white faces from Warhol's film are projected against a wall. The Velvet Underground and dancers blur above two sentences from Joyce's *Finnegans Wake*: "History as she is harped. Rite words in rote order."[50] McLuhan follows those pages with words that recall Ong: "We are enveloped by sound. It forms a seamless web around us."[51]

High and low, sacred and mundane, immediate and eternal: paradox is central to Catholic storytelling and art, since God is perceived in all things. Warhol was one of its finest visual prophets. At Warhol's memorial service, the art historian John Richardson pulled back the veil: Warhol was a devout Catholic, and his faith was "the key to the artist's psyche."[52] He went to daily

Mass at the Church of St. Vincent Ferrer in New York. "Never take Andy at face value," Richardson explained. "The callous observer was in fact a recording angel."[53]

Warhol surrounded himself with Catholic artists, photographers, poets and managers: Fred Hughes, Gerald Malanga, Paul Morrissey, Bob Colacello, Natasha Fraser-Cavassoni, Christopher Makos, Robert Mapplethorpe, and Vincent Fremont. The same year he created the "Exploding Plastic Inevitable" spectacles, Warhol created a silkscreen series of Marilyn Monroe. The portfolio's varying shades and colors take an endlessly recycled face and imbue transformative life. There is something vaguely liturgical in Warhol's recursive method.

This is not to say that such pop work was devotional; Warhol saved that for his Last Supper sequence. Alexandre Iolas commissioned Warhol to create a series based on Leonardo da Vinci's famous work. For an artist who had made the mundane mystical—think soup cans and soda bottles—this was a different context. It was a print masterpiece resurrected, an artistic word made flesh, draped in camouflage, silkscreened, infused with layers of pop and piety. Warhol created over one hundred takes on Leonardo's creation, his repetition suffused with the rhythm of prayer. Somewhere between Warhol's public glam and his private, blue-collar Catholicism rested a spirit similar to the "inscape" of the poet Gerard Manley Hopkins, the belief that even the most mundane and artificial objects exist in a divine world.

McLuhan, Ong, and Warhol watched the electronic age arrive and found eternal patterns, moments of illumination, a new opportunity for communion, clarity and mysticism. God truly was in the machine. In *The Crying of Lot 49*, Pynchon created a psychotropic world that is part parody, part paean to an intense theological system. Catholicism and its sensory rituals, dramatic stories, and almost labyrinthine sense of hierarchy attracted Pynchon's appetite for intrigue. He channels the energy and elements of McLuhan, Ong, and Warhol, but pivots away from their piety.

A global postal conspiracy. Post horns graffitied across Southern California. LSD prescribed as treatment for anxiety. Obscene radio station hosts. Beatles cover bands. Widespread paranoia. *The Crying of Lot 49* is quirky and eccentric even by Pynchon's standards. The novel is truly a snapshot of mid-1960s Southern California culture, saturated with the cultural minutia and noise of that moment.

Oedipa Maas is the protagonist that McLuhan might dream of, a woman thrust into an electronic world she did not create but is forced to understand. Early in the novel, Oedipa and Metzger, her part-time lover, part-time legal mentor, visit The Scope, a nightclub on the outskirts of Los Angeles with "a strictly electronic music policy."[54] A "hip graybeard" explains "They put it on the tape, here, live, fella. We've got a whole back room full of your audio oscillators, gunshot machines, contact mikes, everything man."[55] As Oedipa drives through San Narciso on a Sunday, "She looked down a slope, needing to squint for the sunlight, onto a vast sprawl of houses which had grown up all together, like a well-tended crop, from the dull brown earth; and she thought of the time she'd opened a transistor radio to replace a battery and seen her first printed circuit."[56] Oedipa's world is wholly electronic; in fact, considering Pynchon's sensibility as a jester-Catholic, holy electronic.

Oedipa Maas seeks meaning in a confusing world. She begins the novel in a mystically domestic moment, standing "in the living room, stared at by the greenish dead eye of the TV tube, spoke the name of God, tried to feel as drunk as possible."[57] She has just been named executrix of the estate of her millionaire ex-boyfriend,

Pierce Inverarity, who had a penchant for prank phone calls and financing the military-industrial complex.

Oedipa is stirred by this development, but not quite shaken. Pynchon might throw Oedipa into a world she did not create, but he does so by arming her and disarming the men who surround her.

While Pynchon has been placed firmly into the masculine canon of the previous century, Oedipa is his breakout character: a woman who, against all odds, strives to remake the world into a place of meaning and structure. It is the men in Pynchon's California who are secondary: they are duplicitous, flighty, and weak. Mucho, Oedipa's husband, is a pervert disk jockey who could not "use honey to sweeten his coffee for like all things viscous it distressed him."[58] Roseman, a lawyer-friend, "tried to play footsie with her under the table" but Oedipa "was wearing boots, and couldn't feel much of anything."[59] Another lawyer, former child-actor Metzger, wants to play a form of strip poker, so Oedipa drowns herself in clothing: "six pairs of panties in assorted colors, girdle, three pairs of nylons, three brassieres, two pairs stretch slacks, four half-slips, one black sheath, two summer dresses, half dozen A-line skirts, three sweaters, two blouses, quilted wrapper, baby blue peignoir and old Orlon muu-muu."[60]

There's depth beneath this silly surface. Early in the novel, Oedipa returns to San Narciso to examine Pierce's books and records. Pynchon puts her in a rented Impala on a Sunday afternoon, and she pauses like God at the top of a hill. She looks down at the streets and compares them to the circuit of a transistor radio, considering that "there were to both outward patterns a hieroglyphic sense of concealed meaning, of an intent to communicate."[61] Oedipa is a character who can both become enthralled by "this illusion of speed, freedom, wind in your hair, unreeling landscape"—yet recognize that "it wasn't."[62] Rather, this industrial-suburbia road was a "hypodermic needle, inserted somewhere ahead into the vein of a freeway, a vein nourishing the mainliner LA, keeping it happy, coherent, protected from pain, or whatever passes, with a city, for pain."[63]

Oedipa's pain is her constant worry that Pierce has manufactured a game for her, that her will has been, quite literally, bent toward his will. This might suggest another clichéd female character manipulated by a man, but the novel is more complicated than that. Oedipa is neither romanticized nor sexualized; in fact, her sexuality is a source of power. Thrust into the shadow of Trystero, a multinational postal conspiracy, she doesn't waver. She fights.

At the end of the book, Oedipa tries to sort the noise of her life. She is not sure whether Pierce "encrypted" Trystero into the will so that Oedipa would discover it, or if she had discovered it by accident. Her search is not the vacuity of empty paranoia. Pynchon is again lyric: "For it was now like walking among matrices of a great digital computer, the zeroes and ones twinned above, hanging like balanced mobiles right and left, ahead, think, maybe endless. Behind the hieroglyphic streets there would either be a transcendent meaning, or only the earth."[64] Oedipa resigns herself to the fact that "there either was some Trystero beyond the appearance of the legacy America, or there was just America and if there was just America then it seemed the only way she could continue, and manage to be at all relevant to it, was as alien, unfurrowed, assumed full circle into some paranoia."[65] Pynchon offers that both might be possible: Oedipa could be paranoid *and* prescient.

Whether or not Oedipa discovers conventional meaning at the end of the novel is besides the point. Her character is active, discerning, as much a part of the "game" as the dead man behind the curtain. In his second novel, Pynchon updates the wild world of *V.* into endlessly replicating conspiracy. Oedipa's search for personal and spiritual meaning in the novel is muddled by the sheer amount of contemporary references, from Tupperware to *Perry Mason* to The Paranoids, a parody of the Beatles. The information entropy of the text matches the acronym of W.A.S.T.E., an underground mail-delivery system that appears connected with Trystero. Oedipa follows every lead, however absurd, with an almost religious devotion (she tries to track down the original script of a pornographic Jacobean revenge play for mention of Trystero, leading another character to ask, "Why is everybody so interested in texts?").[66] Words and signs are delivered outside of accepted channels, and like her husband Mucho's used car lot, they result in "residue" and "loss."

In the entropic world of *The Crying of Lot 49*, Oedipa seeks to become a "sensitive": literally, a psychic who can help sort molecules in a Demon Box, and metaphorically, a woman who can sort through the noise of misinformation to discern the true scope of Trystero. Although she fails at the literal application of the concept, her metaphorical pursuit of the truth is akin to a religious pilgrimage. Along the way, everybody seems out to get Oedipa, but unlike the men in her world, she doesn't cower. She barrels headlong into a conspiracy that formed long before she was born, a conspiracy that appears to have taken a particular interest in this suburban housewife from Southern California.

Oedipa's search is fueled by a religious sense of devotion: the ardent belief that the patterns of the world reveal a grand design. One theory goes that Oedipa was chosen because her husband is a disk jockey, someone who "transmits" his own form of noise on the radio, and therefore gives Trystero a wide frequency. Yet, as the novel progresses, it becomes possible that Oedipa's will might even transcend that of her mysterious ex-boyfriend; that it is *she* who has chosen Trystero. Pynchon has created a character who not only seeks but embraces the ambiguity of her world. Even though Oedipa is unable to find the meaning of her life, she does not conclude that life is meaningless. *The Crying of Lot 49*, then, is a book of searching, a book of faith. Oedipa acts on the faith that not only do words matter, but that there is a Word, and that texts can lead her there. That she does not find what she seeks does not devalue the search—and here Pynchon, like McLuhan, is concerned with the process of searching for connectivity and communion.

Pynchon would continue that search in a sequence of novels with increasing length and scope. His 1974 novel, *Gravity's Rainbow*, won the National Book Award, and begins with a morbid opening scene of London's evacuation during World War II: "Underfoot crunches the oldest of city dirt, last crystallizations of all the city had denied, threatened, lied to its children."[67] In the dream of Captain Pirate Prentice, a British Special Operations Executive, "There is no way out. Lie and wait, lie still and be quiet. Screaming holds across the sky. When it comes, will it come in darkness, or will it bring its own light? Will the light come before or after?"[68]

After *Vineland* (1990), a punchy novel set in California and starring aging 60s-era hippies, Pynchon returned to a novel of historical expanse in *Mason & Dixon* (1997). The fictional take on the eighteenth century pair of British surveyors is told by a Reverend Cherrycoke, who seems less than reliable. Pynchon includes excerpts from the preacher's *Undeliver'd Sermons*: "Doubt is of the essence of Christ. . . . The final pure Christ is pure uncertainty. He is become the central subjunctive fact of a Faith, that risks ev'rything upon one bodily Resurrection. . . . Wouldn't something less doubtable have done? a prophetic dream, a communication with a dead person?"[69]

The novel includes a winding subplot with Jesuits—Pynchon's go-to religious order. As with DeLillo, Jesuits for Pynchon represent an intellectual, conspiratorial, shadow subgenre of Catholicism—a multinational, influential group that is pious, ambitious, and powerful. Erudite and obsessed with texts, Pynchon's Jesuits are postmodern priests, capable of channeling mysticism, yet grounded in language. Pynchon, consistent with his satirist tone, exaggerates "to parodic levels every perfidy of which Jesuits were presumed capable.[70] Since Pynchon's works are often pastiches of genres—historical fiction, detective stories, war novels—it is appropriate that he plays up stereotypes for subversive purposes.

A search for postmodern sincerity is a dangerous game, especially one played with a master such as Pynchon, but his Catholic years create a tantalizing paradox. The fact remains that one of America's most heralded and complex contemporary novelists was not merely once a practicing Catholic, but one who remains fascinated with its theology, its ethical questions, and even its religious orders. His initial breakthrough as a writer occurred during a decade of Catholic intellectual and artistic innovation. Pynchon admired McLuhan and played similar games as Warhol—albeit with different mediums. Their shared religious interests and influences suggest that there are certain traits of Catholicism—its coupling of grandeur with the corporal and visceral; its offering of a complex theological map for a world that seems increasingly absurd—that makes it strangely appropriate for a postmodern world.

The answer, as it often is with Pynchon, is less important than the question, and the question is often hidden. In 1984, as part of the publication push for *Slow Learner*, Pynchon wrote an essay for *The New York Times Book Review*. "Is It OK to Be a Luddite?" is a whimsical take on the historical and legendary background for our colloquial usage of the term and offers Pynchon the opportunity to argue that we should best consider Luddites as an economic, populist revolution, rather than a band of maniacs.

Yet it is an essay published there nearly a decade later that is more enticing. The book review's editors asked a handful of contemporary writers to consider the seven deadly sins. Gore Vidal took on pride. Mary Gordon investigated anger. John Updike, unsurprisingly, examined lust. Thomas Pynchon was asked to ponder sloth.

Pynchon begins by talking about the profoundly influential thirteenth century priest, theologian, and saint, Thomas Aquinas. He quips that Aquinas was a bit harsh in labeling sloth as a capital, or mortal, sin. "Writers are considered the mavens of Sloth"—with procrastination being part of the profession.[71] *Acedia*, the Latin word used by Aquinas for the condition, means sorrow, "deliberately self-directed, turned away from God, a loss of spiritual determination."[72] Considering the social and literary history of America, Pynchon sees the concept of acedia as shifting "from a spiritual to a secular condition."[73]

Modern America—the audience for which Pynchon writes, and about whom he has often written—is defined by sloth. "Acedia," he argues, "is the vernacular of everyday moral life."[74] Modern sloth is "despair bought at a discount price, a deliberate turning against faith in anything because of the inconvenience faith presents to the pursuit of quotidian lusts, angers and the rest."[75] Pynchon wonders if anyone cares. "Unless the state of our souls becomes once more a subject of serious concern, there is little question that Sloth will continue to evolve away from its origins in the long-ago age of faith and miracle, when daily life really was the Holy Ghost visibly at work and time was a story, with a beginning, middle and end."[76]

Pynchon's tone is difficult to discern here. The ultimate trick of the literary jester is surprise; we expect comedy, which makes sincerity easy to miss. For a writer often considered a paranoid satirist who laughs at the world, Thomas Pynchon finds much in it to lament. His fiction is a confluence of his Catholic contemporaries. Within Pynchon's complex plots and eccentric characters, we find McLuhan's theories of the electronic world, Ong's perception of our place within the sensorium, and Warhol's sacral, contemplative core beneath his performative absurdity. Pynchon offers his readers a psychotropic Catholic vision, making us feel much like Oedipa Maas at the end of her quest—attending an auction that will hopefully contain the revelation of history's secrets, and watching the auctioneer "spread his arms in a gesture that seemed to belong to the priesthood of some remote culture; perhaps to a descending angel."[77] In Pynchon's fiction, God may or may not be revealed, but the spectacle remains.

5

A STORY OF THE BODY

Toni Morrison

Cornel West, the philosopher and professor, leaned forward, gripping the edges of the podium. He stood in the dining room of Maryhouse, the Catholic Worker home where the activist and journalist Dorothy Day spent the final years of her life—ill, her writing greatly slowed, and yet still in prayer. West was speaking in November 2012, on the occasion of her 116th birthday, and his address documented Day's legacy, her verve, and her spirit:

> Dorothy reminds me in so many ways of Toni Morrison. You know Toni Morrison is Catholic. Many people do not realize that she is one of the great Catholic writers. Like Flannery O'Connor, she has an incarnational conception of human existence. We Protestants are too individualistic. I think we need to learn from Catholics who are always centered on community.

The 1993 recipient of the Nobel Prize in Literature, Toni Morrison converted to Catholicism in 1943, while a twelve-year-old student at Hawthorne Junior High School in Lorain, Ohio. Named Chloe at birth, she took the name of St. Anthony of Padua. Her nickname soon became Toni. Her mother, Ramah Wofford, was "a devout member of the African Methodist Episcopal Church."[1] Yet Morrison recalls "there's a wing of my family who are all Catholics."[2] She was very close with a Catholic cousin, which in part led to her baptism into the church.

As a teenager, Morrison was "perfectly content" with the "aesthetics" of Catholicism.[3] For Morrison, religion was very much a place of story and art. She loved her mother's singing voice, so Morrison conceived of her mother's Christian faith through the particular prayer of song. In a similar way, Morrison became a Catholic because of its sense of story and visuals. "That's shallow," she once joked in an interview on NPR. "But that's what it was, until I grew up a little older and began to take it seriously and then took it seriously for years and years and years."[4]

Morrison is a storyteller shaped by a Catholic faith based in visceral narrative, and yet West is correct that many people do not realize she is a Catholic. It is not quite an act of willful ignorance on the part of critics and readers although Morrison has never shied from framing her sense of story, thought, and belief within a Catholic worldview.

In a 2004 appearance at The Nation Institute, Morrison and West discussed the intersection of Christianity and political discourse. Their conversation veered toward the recently-released film *The Passion of the Christ*. Based on the trailer and the marketing, West stayed away from the film. Morrison, though, had gone to see it with a friend.

"Now, you know, I'm a Catholic," she says. "We're used to blood and gore. On the cross in the church, there's the body, with the cuts and the bruises. Protestant churches: nice, clean cross. No body at all." The film's depiction of the Passion narrative, then, was nothing new for Morrison; as a young convert drawn to story and image, she would be especially amenable to that most dramatic sequence. Yet she thought the film's "bloodiness was uninteresting, excessive, repulsive." She even admitted that she fell asleep.

Morrison and West laughed along with the audience, but she then describes what happened next during her viewing. Although she felt the film did not ultimately succeed on its own merits, it was generative for her—she responded to the images that repulsed her. She tried to understand the film through her own Catholic theology, and reflected that the Passion wasn't about "merely the Spirit, this really was about the flesh . . . and we forget that. This is real suffering. I was looking at it like a lynching . . . this is a betrayed man who is hung, lynched."

The year before this conversation at The National Institute, Morrison was quoted in *The Washington Post* identifying as a "disaffected Catholic." In 2007, her religious identity would be even more enigmatic. In a fascinating, blunt interview with Italian film director Antonio Monda, Morrison speaks very much as a lapsed Catholic—not merely distanced from the institutional church, but open to an idiosyncratic theology, a set of beliefs of her own making.

When asked if she believes in God, she says "I believe in an intelligence interested in what exists and respectful of what is created."[5] Belief in God is, itself, "an intellectual experience that intensifies our perceptions and distances us from an egocentric and predatory life, from ignorance and from the limits of personal satisfactions."[6] Here her conception of God sounds only vaguely

Christian, but she reaffirms her attraction to, and fascination with, Catholic ritual, and even offers what she calls a "surprise" to the interviewer. "I had a moment of crisis on the occasion of Vatican II," she says. "At the time I had the impression that it was a superficial change, and I suffered greatly from the abolition of Latin, which I saw as the unifying and universal language of the Church. But I still find the revolution of love that replaced the idea of justice astonishing. It's something extremely modern, and perhaps eternal, which someone brought to humanity."[7]

Morrison sees a problematic absence of authentic religion in modern art: "It's not serious—it's supermarket religion, a spiritual Disneyland of false fear and pleasure."[8] She laments that religion is often parodied or simplified, as in "those pretentious bad films in which angels appear as dei ex machina, or of figurative artists who use religious iconography with the sole purpose of creating a scandal."[9] She admires the work of James Joyce, especially his earlier works, and has a particular affinity for Flannery O'Connor, "a great artist who hasn't received the attention she deserves."[10]

What emerges from Morrison's public discussions of faith is paradoxical Catholicism. Her conception of God is malleable, progressive, and esoteric. She retains a distinct nostalgia for Catholic ritual, and feels the "greatest respect" for those who practice the faith, even if she herself has wavered.[11] In a 2015 interview with NPR, Morrison said there was not a "structured" sense of religion in her life at the moment, but "I might be easily seduced to go back to church because I like the controversy as well as the beauty of this particular Pope Francis. He's very interesting to me."[12]

Morrison's Catholic faith—past and present, individual and communal, traditional and idiosyncratic—offers a theological structure for her worldview. Her Catholicism illuminates her fiction, in particular, her views of bodies and the narrative power of stories. In a broader sense, she adopts a consistently Christian view of the role of an artist in a society and the role of a novelist as it relates to her subjects.

An artist, Morrison affirms, "bears witness."[13] She was raised on her father's ghost stories, and notes, "I am very superstitious."[14] Her family's religious sense was an amalgam; while they "talked a great deal about Jesus—they selected out of Christianity all the things they felt applicable to their situation—but they also kept this other body of knowledge that we call superstitious."[15] Her father's ghost stories, her mother's spiritual musicality, and her own youthful sense of attraction to Christianity's "scriptures and its vagueness" leads her to conclude Christianity is "a theatrical religion. It says something particularly interesting to black people, and I think it's part of why they were so available to it. It was the love things that were psychically very important. Nobody could have endured that life in constant rage."[16] Morrison says it is a sense of "transcending love" that makes "the New Testament . . . so pertinent to black literature—the lamb, the victim, the vulnerable one who does die but nevertheless lives."[17]

"It's always seemed to me," Morrison says, "that black people's grace has been with what they do with language,"[18] and this writing is very much "in touch with the magic and the mystery and the things of the body."[19] The body, as Morrison knows, is a place of extreme emotions—a literary place of risk. Rather than approach the body with caution, Morrison likes "the danger in writing when you're right on the edge, when at any moment you can be maudlin, saccharine, grotesque, but somehow pull back from it."[20] Morrison is describing a Catholic style of storytelling here, reflected in the various emotional notes of Mass. The religion calls for extremes: solemnity, joy, silence, and exhortation. Such a literary approach is audacious, confident, and necessary, considering Morrison's broader goals. She rejects the term experimental, clarifying "I am simply trying to recreate something out of an old art form in my books—the something that defines what makes a book 'black.'"[21]

What makes a book "black," for Morrison, are unique elements of language, narrative, and religion. She says black stories "are just told—meanderingly—as though they are going in several directions at the same time."[22] Those directions are built upon tradition and structure; black literary style is defined by "cleaning up the language so that old words have new meanings. It has a spine that's very biblical and meandering and aural—you really have to hear it."[23]

Morrison is both storyteller and archivist. Her commitment to history and tradition itself feels Catholic in orientation. She seeks to "merge vernacular with the lyric, with the standard, and with the biblical, because it was part of the linguistic heritage of my family, moving up and down the scale, across it, in between it."[24] When a serious subject came up in family conversation, "it was highly sermonic, highly formalized, biblical in a sense, and easily so. They could move easily into the language of the King James Bible and then back to standard English, and then segue into language that we would call street."

Language was play and performance; the pivots and turns were "an enhancement for me, not a restriction," and showed her that "there was an enormous power" in such shifts.[25] Morrison's attention toward language is inherently religious; by talking about the change from Latin to English Mass as a regrettable shift, she invokes the sense that faith is both content and language—both story and medium.

Morrison's youthful love for language led her to study English and classics at Howard University, followed by a master's degree in English literature from Cornell University in 1955. Her thesis was titled *Virginia Woolf's and William Faulkner's Treatment of the Alienated*. She taught for several years at Texas Southern University and at Howard, and then began a formidable publishing career at Random House—first as a textbook editor, and later as editor and champion of black writers, including Toni Cade Bambara and James Alan McPherson.

Her own debut novel was published in 1970. *The Bluest Eye* is the story of Pecola Breedlove, an eleven-year-old girl in Lorain, Ohio. One of the first prologue chapters of the novel includes a scene collectively narrated by Claudia and Frieda MacTeer, sisters who hope for two things: that the marigold seeds they've planted in the ground will grow, and that Pecola's child would survive. In the first pages of the novel, we learn that neither prayer is answered, so the story arrives with a disclaimer: *"There is really nothing more to say—except why. But since why is difficult to handle, one must take refuge in how."*[26]

The narrative proper begins in a slightly surreal manner: "Nuns go by as quiet as lust, and drunken men and sober eyes sing in the lobby of the Greek hotel."[27] Claudia and Frieda live in their own world while "Grown-ups talk in tired, edgy voices."[28] In their "old, cold, and green house," the girls listen to the particular song of speech that surrounds them.[29] Although the young sisters are dismissed by the adults—spoken to, rather than spoken with—the girls love to listen to the conversations of their elders. The speech of adults "is like a gently wicked dance: sound meets sound, curtsies, shimmies, and retires."[30] The words are "punctuated with warm-pulsed laughter—like the throb of a heart made of jelly."[31] The girls don't understand much of the content, but "we watch their faces, their hands, their feet, and listen for truth in timbre."[32]

The sisters narrate their world with a sense of wonder. They cross town to collect stray coal from the railroad tracks. "Later we walk home, glancing back to see the great carloads of slag being dumped, red hot and smoking, into the ravine that skirts the steel mill. The dying fire lights the sky with a dull orange glow."[33] After one trip, Claudia coughs "loudly, through bronchial tubes already packed tight with phlegm."[34] Sick and delirious, she is cared for by her mother: "Love, thick and dark as Alaga syrup, eased up into that cracked window."[35]

Into this world arrives Pecola, a "case"—a young girl whose broken home life led the county to place her in the MacTeer house.[36] The Breedloves previously lived in a storefront "because they were poor and black, and they stayed there because they believed they were ugly."[37] The novel's often unforgiving third person narrated chapters offer context and explanation and feel like the judgmental eyes of society. Pauline and Cholly Breedlove's marriage was destined for struggle. She was an "upright and Christian woman, burdened with a no-count man, whom God wanted her to punish."[38] Stoic and stubborn, she held her husband "as a model of sin and failure, she bore him like a crown of thorns, and her children like a cross."[39]

Pauline's thoughts upon Pecola's birth are striking: "*Head full of pretty hair, but Lord she was ugly.*"[8] Pecola hated her blackness, and would pray every night for blue eyes so that she would no longer feel ugly. Her self-hatred comes from the fury in her home, but also how the world looks at her: "The distaste must be for her, her blackness . . . blackness is static and dread. And it is the blackness that accounts for, that creates, the vacuum edged with distaste in white eyes."[40]

Yet unlike Pecola, the MacTeer girls do not desire blue eyes. In one of Claudia's narrated chapters, she observes that "Adults, older girls, shops, magazines, newspapers, window signs—all the world had agreed that a blue-eyed, yellow-haired, pink-skinned doll was what every girl treasured."[41] Not Claudia. She wanted to dismember a blue-eyed doll, and carried that hatred to white girls—but that hatred was equal parts revulsion and fascination, a desire "to discover what eluded me: the secret of the magic they weaved on others."[42]

Early in her stay with them, Pecola menstruates, causing the girls to be "full of awe and respect" for her.[43] Her coming pregnancy has a horrific origin: she was raped by her father, Cholly. The scene spans several pages, and remains difficult and shocking to read, years after its original publication. Morrison chooses to represent evil directly, and viscerally—so that the act is not neutered by rumor or anecdote.

When the sisters finally learn the origin of Pecola's pregnancy, their "sorrow was the more intense because nobody else seemed to share it."[44] Others in town "were disgusted, amused, shocked, outraged, or even excited by the story."[45] Claudia, especially, was distraught. "More strongly than my fondness for Pecola," she admits, "I felt a need for someone to want the black baby to live."[46]

Years later, Pecola lives with her mother "on the edge of town," where she is "picking and plucking her way between the tire rims and the sunflowers, between Coke bottles and milkweed, among all the waste and beauty of the world—which is what she herself was. All of our waste which we dumped on her and which she absorbed. And all of our beauty, which was hers first and which she gave to us."[47] The novel's final section is riddled with guilt. Pecola's baby did not survive, and the girls come to terms with Pecola's tragedies. "We were so beautiful when we stood astride her ugliness," Claudia says—an indictment of themselves but also the society that looked at Pecola and her family as disposable.[48]

The Bluest Eye suggests that the stories that are difficult to handle are often told in vague and abstract ways; that language has the power to vanish these unsightly stories. Soon after Cholly's attack of Pecola, there is a lyrically narrated section by Claudia: "I have only to break into the tightness of a strawberry, and I see summer—its dust and lowering skies."[49] She imagines how her mother felt in Lorain, Ohio, in 1929, a "slim young girl in a pink crepe dress," as the "wind swoops her up, high above the houses, but she is still standing, hand on hip."[50] From her first novel on forward, Morrison appears intent on forcing us to look at embodied black pain with the full power of language. As a Catholic writer, she wants us to see the body on the cross; to see its blood, its cuts, its sweat.

Although several novels would follow—*Sula* (1973), *Song of Solomon* (1977), *Tar Baby* (1981)—*The Bluest Eye* feels most connected to *Beloved* (1988), perhaps Morrison's most ambitious, stirring work. "Black people never annihilate evil," Morrison has said. "They don't run it out of their neighborhoods, chop it up, or burn it up. They don't have witch hangings. They accept it. It's almost like a fourth dimension in their lives."[51] *Beloved* is a ghost story. A tale of evil, superstition, and phantasmagoria. The present action of the novel takes place in 1873, in Cincinnati, Ohio, at a home on Bluestone Road. Sethe, the main character, has escaped slavery at the Sweet Home plantation to reach this house, but there is no peace there. 124 Bluestone Road is "spiteful," and "full of a baby's venom."[52] Mirrors shatter. A baby's handprints appear in a cake. Chickpeas, smoking, pile on the floor. A trail of crumbled soda crackers leads to the doorsill. Sethe's sons, Howard and Bugler, have run away, leaving Sethe with her mother (who dies soon after), and her daughter, Denver.

Sethe had wanted to move, but her mother reminded her that there's "Not a house in the country ain't packed to its rafters with some dead Negro's grief."[53] Her mother's words are painfully literal. As with *The Bluest Eye*, we learn the secrets of *Beloved* early. Sethe had killed her infant child. Afraid that her young daughter would be caught and brought back to slavery, Sethe killed her in a shed—a hideously public act that makes Sethe an infamous, almost mythic, figure. The murder is shocking, heartbreaking, inconceivable; a permutation of Cholly's horrid act in *The Bluest Eye*.

Slavery—the bondage and ownership of bodies and the suffering of souls—is the prototypical American sin for Morrison, and from the first page of *Beloved*, the story is focused on what happens when past sins bleed into the present and take corporal form. Sethe tries to conjure the spirit that haunts the house, but it does not answer. "You forgetting how little it is," Sethe says to her daughter, Denver. "She wasn't even two years old when she died."[54]

Paul D, the last man remaining from the Sweet Home plantation, arrives at the house. Sethe invites him inside, but he is nervous: "What kind of evil you got in here?"[55] He feels "soaked" by grief in the house.[56] Inside, before he first sees Denver, the space is described in an ethereal, and haunting, way: "The luminous white of the railing and steps kept him glancing toward it. Every sense he had told him the air above the stairwell was charmed and very thin. But the girl who walked down out of that air was round and brown with the face of an alert doll."[57]

Paul D says they should leave the house, but Sethe won't: "No more running—from nothing."[58] Denver doesn't want to leave either; she "wished for the baby ghost—its anger thrilling her now where it used to wear her out."[59] Denver recalls seeing Sethe "on her knees in prayer" and a "white dress knelt down next to her mother and had its sleeve around her mother's waist."[60]

Sethe says that she wasn't praying: "I don't pray anymore. I just talk."[61] Sethe often speaks of memory as being permanent, physical. She says nothing ever dies. 124 has become a conduit; its physical walls are another body for the baby, now ghost. Denver's prediction is simple: "the baby got plans."[62]

Paul D's arrival, carrying the past with him, further disrupts the boundaries of time, of the real and unreal, and forces the ghost's plans into actions. When Paul D tries to be close to Sethe and hug her, the floorboards begin to shake. A table bursts toward him; he smashes it, and was "screaming back at the screaming house."[63] Undaunted, Paul D says they can make a life together. They go to a carnival in town, and "were not holding hands, but their shadows were."[64] Denver, sullen for so long, was "swaying with delight."[65]

On the next page, the character of Beloved first appears: "A fully dressed woman walked out of the water."[66] A ghost made flesh. Beloved emerges from a stream and leans against a mulberry tree. She sits there all day and night. Her whole body is in pain, especially her lungs. Soaked, her breaths wheeze like asthma, yet she still smiles. Her skin is "lineless and smooth."[67] A day later, she walks through the woods and sits on a stump near the steps of 124. She passes in and out of sleep, her neck bending. Her arrival is audacious, miraculous.

Sethe, Denver, and Paul D return home from the carnival, and see Beloved for the first time. The "rays of the sun struck her full in the face" so that "all they saw was a black dress, two unlaced shoes below it."[68] Denver tells them to look, saying "What is that?"; notably not "who" is that.[69] They take Beloved inside, where she drinks four glasses of water. She says her name is Beloved, her voice "so low and rough."[70]

Morrison has said that all of her writing is "about love or its absence."[71] There must always be one or the other—her characters do not live without ebullience or suffering. "Black women," Morrison explains, "have held, have been given, you know, the cross. They don't walk near it. They're often on it. And they've borne that, I think, extremely well."[72] No character in Morrison's canon lives the cross as much as Sethe, who even "got a tree on my back" from whipping.[73] Scarred inside and out, she is the living embodiment of bearing witness.

Beloved, Sethe's own body, has returned. Beloved sleeps for four days, and awakens only to drink water. Then she pines for sugar: honey, wax, molasses, lemonade, taffy, cane sticks. She can barely walk, but can somehow lift a chair with ease. Her energy is directed toward one person: "Sethe was licked, tasted, eaten by Beloved's eyes."[74] Beloved loves when Sethe tells her stories of the past. She said she had walked a long way there; she's specifically come for 124.

Paul D is suspicious of Beloved, but Sethe feels flattered and loved. She's not the only one. Denver becomes obsessed with Beloved and wants to be with her constantly. Beloved dances; she speaks of being in the grave. She becomes ecstatic, incantational. "She is the one," Beloved says of Sethe. "She is the one I need."[75]

Sethe takes Denver and Beloved to the Clearing, a spot in the woods where her own mother, Baby Suggs, held services. Her mother was an "unchurched preacher."[76] She led people to the Clearing on Saturday afternoons. The congregation would become ecstatic: laugh, cry, dance, and then, "exhausted and riven," they would listen to Baby Suggs preach.[77] Rather than chastise them for sin, she told the people to love their flesh.

Sethe's own flesh, it seems, is in danger. At the Clearing she feels a hand around her neck, possibly strangling her. Is it Beloved? Morrison writes with enough prosaic detail that even in the midst of her supernatural novel, we push aside doubt. Beloved's body is wavering. She pulls out a tooth, and then thinks: "This is it. Next would be her arm, her hand, a toe. Pieces of her would drop maybe one at a time, maybe all at once."[78] She is jealous of Sethe's affection for Paul D, but when he learns from a newspaper clipping that Sethe killed her child, he leaves 124. The women are finally alone.

Morrison, aware of our longing for hope, gives us just enough of that gift through language. While Beloved and Denver are ice skating at a creek: "The sky above them was another country. Winter stars, close enough to lick, had come out before sunset."[79] Yet the old stories and scars remain, and must be dealt with; within the final quarter of the book, the narrative perspective shifts from third person to a vacillating first person. Here Sethe tells her story directly, explaining why—years ago when she was on the run from her slave masters—she killed her child in the shed: "My plan was to take us all to the other side where my own ma'am is. They stopped me from getting us there, but they didn't stop you from getting here."[80] Beloved herself has a chapter of fragmented narrative; a jangle of memories and events, including a refrain of "I am not dead I am not."[81]

The novel's third and climactic section begins with the sentence "124 was quiet," completing an evolution: the home has been spiteful, loud, and now silent.[82] Sethe starts showing up late to work and loses her job. She sees a scar on Beloved's neck—where she'd cut her years ago—and she becomes even closer with Beloved, pushing Denver aside. They are mother and daughter anew, and Beloved "never got enough of anything: lullabies, new stitches, the bottom of the cake bowl, the top of the milk."[83] Beloved wears Sethe's dresses and imitates how her mother "moved her hands, sighed through her nose, held her head."[84]

As they grow even closer, they almost transform into sisters. Affection becomes agitation. Beloved makes Sethe feel guilty for her past sin. She tells Sethe that "when she cried there was no one. That dead men lay on top of her. That she had nothing to eat."[85] Beloved breaks a windowpane, throws salt on the floor, and swipes plates from the table. Denver fears Beloved, no longer wanting to protect her. 124 becomes a place of madness. Beloved would claw at her throat, bleeding. "Other times Beloved curled up on the floor, her wrists between her knees, and stayed there for hours."[86] Beloved often seems like the ecstatic, tortured saints that Morrison had learned about as a child. Like Beloved, their presence in this world feels impossible and dizzying.

Sethe's ultimate fear is that Beloved might leave. Now that Paul D. has left, and taken the story of 124 with him, word has spread around town: "Sethe's dead daughter, the one whose throat she cut, had come back to fix her. Sethe was worn down, speckled, dying, spinning, changing shapes and generally bedeviled."[87] In response, a congregation of thirty women go to the home. The women pray, and then sing, in hopes of cleansing 124.

Sethe greets the crowd at the door, holding hands with Beloved. She feels as if her mother's spiritual past at the Clearing has returned to her "with all its heat and simmering leaves, where the voices of women searched for the right combination, the key, the code, the sound that broke the back of words."[88] The cascade of voices "broke over Sethe and she trembled like the baptized in its wash."[89] She lets go of Beloved's hand and enters the crowd. Beloved—the ghost, the spirit made flesh, Sethe's savior and her phantasm, her daughter—disappears. People "forgot her like a bad dream" because "It was not a story to pass on."[90]

Beloved's story might not be spoken, but it enters the bodies of Sethe, Denver, and even 124. In *The Bluest Eye* and *Beloved*, Morrison considers the malleability of time and memory; each thought is a resurrection of the past. For the black men and women of *Beloved*, there is no distance between past and present: their years of slavery are fresh wounds. Breaths of joy are quickly muted. On one hand, it is an unforgiving theology, but Morrison's Catholicism is one of the Passion: of scarred bodies, public execution, and private penance. When Morrison thinks of "the infiniteness of time, I get lost in a mixture of dismay and excitement. I sense the order and harmony that suggest an intelligence, and I discover, with a slight shiver, that my own language becomes evangelical."[91] The more Morrison contemplates the grandness and complexity of life, the more her writing reverts to the Catholic storytelling methods that enthralled her as a child and cultivated her faith. This creates a powerful juxtaposition: a skilled novelist compelled to both abstraction and physicality in her stories. Catholicism, for Morrison, offers a language to connect these differences. Her wavering practice of the religion has not changed its existence as her narrative voice and structure.

Beloved won the Pulitzer Prize, among other awards. Later that year, Morrison would give the Tanner Lecture on Human Values at the University of Michigan, titled "Unspeakable Things Unspoken: the Afro-American Presence in American Literature." She explains that much of the "satisfaction" she has felt in reading Greek tragedy is "its similarity to Afro-American communal structures (the function of song and chorus, the heroic struggle between the claims of community and individual hubris)"—an apt description of *Beloved*.[92] Her broader concern, though, is the literary canon, the idea that select works across history are required reading as foundational texts for culture and thought. "Canon building is Empire building," she writes, and the presence—or absence—of scholarly attention to black literature is disarming but not surprising.[93]

Yet, at the same time, the tendency to frame black literary inclusion in the canon as an action of "discovery" rather than "recovery" is notable. For Morrison, "it is no longer acceptable merely to image us and imagine for us. We have always been imagining ourselves. . . . We are the subjects of our own narratives, witnesses to and participants in our own experience."[94]

An inevitable element of that process is having control over definition rather than being defined. For Morrison, definition is found in narrative: the stories we tell ourselves and others. Her acceptance of Catholicism hinges on its ability to tell a profound and moving story, and she knows that as a black Catholic writer, she has the ability to define that identity for her readers—a Catholic identity that is made of both traditions and new interpretations. Morrison wonders, "other than melanin and subject matter, what, in fact, may make me a black writer?"[95] She returns to the fabric of her language. Its traits include the "rhythm of a familiar, hand-me-down dignity [that] is pulled along by an accretion of detail displayed in a meandering unremarkableness."[96] Syntax that is "highly aural" and "parabolic."[97] The language of Latin Mass—its grandeur, silences, communal participation, coupled with the congregation's performative resurrection of an ancient tongue—offers a foundation for Morrison's meticulous appreciation of language. The language of black writing and the language of Catholicism overlap. Morrison is attracted to language that plays with conventional time, stretched across multiple planes, so that while stories have beginnings, middles, and ends, they are not operating on fixed points.

A decade later, her novel *Paradise* (1997) is a story that spans and bends time, and contains Morrison's most directly Catholic subject matter. Yet the Catholicism is a shadow, a structure, a place of mystery.

Ruby, an all-black town in Oklahoma, was settled in 1950, and chosen for its isolation. Seventeen miles from the town stands the Convent, an elaborate home built by an embezzler. The mansion's original "bisque and rose-tone marble floors segue into teak ones,"[98] and held "princely tubs and sinks."[99] The home was purchased by a group of nuns, although "Catholic churches and schools in Oklahoma were as rare as fish pockets."[100] The nuns "stripped and whitewashed" the walls, and left the tubs and sinks "coolly corrupt."[101]

The nuns used to sell "produce, barbecue sauce, good bread and the hottest peppers in the world."[102] But their focus was education. They converted the gauche dining room into a schoolroom, "where stilled Arapaho girls once sat and learned to forget."[103]

Christ the King School for Native Girls was out of place, and out of mind. Wayward girls like Consolata were taken in, often against their will. In her narrated chapter, Consolata thinks about how Sister Mary Magna and the other sisters would pray in their mysterious Latin, that "gorgeous language made especially for talking to heaven."[104] As the years go on, and the nuns pass away, and the home becomes a boarding house for abused women. Rumors of witchcraft and horrific violence at the home stoke fear in Ruby, and a group of nine men from town come to enact some type of vengeance and justice. The novel opens with their arrival and ambush.

The dramatic storming of the convent is the novel's profluent event, but its religious core resides elsewhere. In Ruby, Reverend Richard Misner, an ambitious young Baptist minister, seeks to sway a town more taken with the traditional preaching of Reverend Senior Pulliam and his Methodist church. After

Pulliam delivers a guest sermon at a wedding and criticizes Misner during the speech, the younger pastor walks to the back of the church and unhooks a cross from the wall. He contemplates the simple, powerful beauty of the cross. It is a sign made by children "in snow, sand or mud."[105] Over time, crosses have been arranged in rocks, scribbled on cave walls, and piled in bones among the fields. Of all the shapes, the "circle was not first, nor was the parallel or the triangle. It was this mark, this, that lay underneath every other."[106] The cross is absolute, essential: "Without this sign, the believer's life was confined to praising God and taking the hits."[107]

On the cross, Christ's body "propped up on these two intersecting lines to which he was attached in a parody of human embrace, fastened to two big sticks that were so convenient, so recognizable, so embedded in consciousness *as consciousness*, being both ordinary and sublime."[108] Morrison remains in the moment, saturating the scene with detail as the cross becomes crucifix, a place of life and death and resurrection. Her description of Christ on the cross captures Misner's sentiment, but also seems to echo her own conception of Christian faith:

> His woolly head alternately rising on his neck and falling toward his chest, the glow of his midnight skin dimmed by dust, streaked by gall, fouled by spit and urine, gone pewter in the hot, dry wind and, finally, as the sun dimmed in shame, as his flesh matched the odd lessening of afternoon light as though it were evening, always sudden in that climate, swallowing him and the other death row felons, and the silhouette of this original sin merged with a false night sky.[109]

Rather than delivering a sermon of words, Misner holds up the cross to the congregation. He wants the crowd to know of Christ: "He *is* you."[110]

Morrison's representations of faith—believers, doubters, preachers, heretics, and miracles—are powerful because of her evocative language, and also because she presents them without irony. She takes religion seriously. In 2015, Morrison told *The Wall Street Journal* "I am a lapsed Catholic, but Pope Francis is impressive enough to make me reconsider my error."[111] She tends to be self-effacing when describing her own belief, and it feels like an action of humility. In a 2014 interview, she affirmed "I am a Catholic" while explaining her willingness to write with a certain frank, moral clarity in her fiction.[112] Morrison is not being contradictory; she is speaking with nuance. She might be lapsed in practice, but she is culturally—and therefore socially, morally—Catholic.

Although *Paradise* is her only novel to contain explicitly Catholic situations and characters, the bodily anxiety of *The Bluest Eye* and *Beloved* are best understood from a Catholic perspective of the body as a source of grace, sin, and suffering. Pecola's life is what happens when we do not extend love to all people; when families and society fail a young girl. In a similar way, Sethe's body is burned and scarred—a place of sacrilege. Beloved, in contrast, is both flesh and spirit, and her presence makes mundane spaces— 124, streams, the woods—sacred locations. The same aesthetics that originally attracted Morrison to Catholicism are revealed in her fiction, despite her wavering of institutional adherence. Her radical approach to the body also makes her the greatest American Catholic writer about race.

That one of the finest, most heralded American writers is Catholic—and yet not spoken about as such—demonstrates why the status of lapsed Catholic writers is so essential to under-standing American fiction. A faith charged with sensory detail, performance, and story, Catholicism seeps into these writers' lives—making it impossible to gauge their moral senses without appreciating how they refract their Catholic pasts. The fiction of lapsed Catholic writers suggests a longing for spiritual meaning and a continued fascination with the language and feeling of faith, absent God or not: a profound struggle that illuminates their stories, and that speaks to their readers.

6

A VIOLENT TESTAMENT

Cormac McCarthy

"I was not what they had in mind," says Cormac McCarthy of his parents.[1] Terse and bluntly comic, McCarthy's self-assessment sounds like it might have come from one of his own characters, hunched over a Texas campfire. The tendency to conflate McCarthy and his brash, independent, southwestern characters hasn't been hurt by the author's popular identity. He doesn't teach, and he doesn't give lectures. He wins awards, but spurns their ceremonies. In dust jacket photos, he wears an open shirt, jeans, and sits against worn brick and wood.

Quite the change for a boy born in Providence, Rhode Island, on July 20, 1933. His father and namesake, Charles Joseph McCarthy, was a Yale-educated lawyer who moved the family to Knoxville, Tennessee in 1937. They lived in a ten-room home with generous land and a staff of maids. "We were considered rich,"

McCarthy reflects, "because all the people around us were living in one or two-room shacks."[2]

They would return to Echo Lake, Rhode Island during the summers, when young McCarthy would take an Old Town canoe on the water, but otherwise his life, and his personal mythology, was defined by Tennessee. He hated school and loved adventure. He went fishing. He chased frogs. He trekked into the woods behind the family home and searched caves. He joined friends on jaunts into Brown's Mountain, his eyes and ears pined for local tales. "You grow in the South," he says, "you're going to see violence."[3] McCarthy was a jokester with an imagination, who loved nature. "I felt early on I wasn't going to be a respectable citizen."[4]

His parents tried to make him one. McCarthy went to Catholic school. First, he attended St. Mary's School on Vine Avenue in Knoxville; the school is right next to the Church of the Immaculate Conception, depicted in his novel *Suttree*. McCarthy was confirmed at that church on January 11, 1942. Then he attended Knoxville Catholic High School, housed in the Gregory Ashe home at 1610 East Magnolia Avenue. Opened by the Sisters of Mercy in 1932, the school had a graduating class of 31 students by the time McCarthy finished his studies.

He studied Latin, and sang in the school choir. His quintet sang at the midnight Mass on Christmas Eve at Immaculate Conception.[5] Young McCarthy—backwoods adventurer, steeped with imagination—would have filled the low-lit church with these words:

> *Dominus dixit ad me:*
> *Filius meus es tu,*
> *ego hodie genui te.*

Quare fremuerunt gentes:
et populi meditati sunt inania?
Gloria Patri, et Filio, et Spiritui Sancto:
Sicut erat in principio, et nunc, et semper,
et in sæcula sæculorum. Amen.

In McCarthy's pre–Vatican II world, the untranslated Latin would have seeped into the walls, although he would have known their meaning:

The Lord hath said to me:

Thou art My Son,
this day have I begotten Thee.

Why have the Gentiles raged,
and the people devised vain things?

Glory be to the Father, and to the Son, and to the Holy Spirit:
As it was in the beginning, is now,
and ever shall be: world without end. Amen.

"I think it embittered him," Bill Kidwell, an old friend, said of McCarthy's Catholicism: "Because of that, he was never fully at peace with his parents. That's directly reflected in *Suttree*, the same story, essentially an autobiography."[6] McCarthy himself has said his childhood Catholicism "wasn't a big issue. We went to church on Sunday. I don't remember religion ever even being discussed."[7] The silver-tongued McCarthy's proclamations should be taken with a pound of salt. In that same interview with the *Wall Street Journal*, McCarthy, straight-faced, said: "I ended up in the Southwest because I knew that nobody had ever written about it. . . . But nobody had taken it seriously, not in 200 years. I thought, here's a good subject. And it was."[8]

His younger brother Bill spent over a decade in a Jesuit seminary in the New Orleans Province, leaving before ordination in 1968.[9] After Cormac McCarthy graduated from Knoxville Catholic in 1951, he drifted from the institutional Church. He went to the University of Tennessee for two years, and studied physics, engineering, and literature, but left to enter the Air Force. He was stationed in Alaska for four years, where he had a radio show for two years, and read widely.

He returned to the University of Tennessee in 1957 and got serious about writing. He published two stories, "Wake for Susan" and "A Drowning Incident," in the school's literary magazine, *The Phoenix*. He won the university's Ingram-Merrill Award for creative writing in both 1959 and 1960, and began writing novels.

He left the school in 1960 without graduating, and began an itinerant life. He finished his first novel, *The Orchard Keeper*, while working a part-time job in an auto-parts warehouse in Chicago. The manuscript was pulled from the slush pile by Random House. The *Virginia Quarterly Review* called McCarthy "a man of infinite promise."[10] *The New York Times* also thought McCarthy "highly gifted," but like some other contemporary novelists of rural country, "sorely handicapped by their humble and excessive admiration for William Faulkner."[11] The next year, McCarthy, appropriately enough, won the annual William Faulkner Foundation award.

McCarthy's career might be distilled into three general periods, whose themes overlap but appear in varied settings and plots. His early works constitute his Appalachian period. This is perhaps his most rangy period, producing visceral, woodsy tales like *Outer Dark*, as well as an urban dark comedy like *Suttree*. These works often draw upon McCarthy's own youth in Tennessee and his manipulations of local folklore and tradition. His second period includes his southwestern novels. Historically inspired but not wedded to actual historical events, these books led to McCarthy's rise in popularity in America and internationally. His third and current period is hardest to define, and might be best thought of as encapsulated by the success of *The Road*—a work that blurs genre lines.

All three periods of McCarthy's fiction include violence, religious symbolism and language, and a bleak tone. Yet, their varying methods and styles imply an evolution of McCarthy's fictional concerns and values. His Appalachian novels are bizarre in action and baroque in language. His southwestern books are mythic. His recent work is sentimental and nostalgic—at least in the McCarthy sense of the words. Taken together, they are an impressive body of work that sets McCarthy apart from his contemporaries. A closer look at each period offers a way to understand how McCarthy has evolved as a Catholic writer.

Beginning with *The Orchard Keeper* (1965), McCarthy's Appalachian works are marked by backwoods violence and eccentric characters. The east Tennessee of his novels is apocryphal, mystical, and downright muddy: a place that exists in a nightmare. *The Orchard Keeper* is a book of revenge, but mostly a story of elegiac transcendence—the melancholy notes of tired lives. McCarthy's novel is not a linear thriller. Vengeance follows a weary road here, a nod toward the novelist's sense that the world is bigger, more complex than one story can capture. Rain and ghostly overcast skies feel frequent in the novel: "Lightning glared in threatful illusions of proximity and quick shapes appeared in the road, leapt from ditch or tree in configurations antic and bizarre. Ghosts of mist rose sadly from the paving and broke in willowy shreds upon the hood, the windshield."[12] McCarthy's flashes of inhuman violence are calmed, but not muted, by his intermittent descriptions of place. It is as if McCarthy wishes to remind his readers of the natural world, one that predates us and will long outlive us.

McCarthy's style differs from Faulkner, his supposed literary precursor. Faulkner's Southern Gothic style is rooted in a nearly Victorian sense of horror; think Miss Emily's decomposed husband in her bridal-like room. McCarthy's early novels capture almost another dimension, some purgatorial wilderness. The final lines of *The Orchard Keeper* capture this sense: "They are gone now. Fled, banished in death or exile, lost, undone. Over the land sun and wind still move to burn and sway the trees, the grasses. No avatar, no scion, no vestige of that people remains. On the lips of the strange race that now dwells there their names are myth, legend, dust."[13]

That ghostly trinity of myth, legend, and dust is perfected in *Outer Dark*, McCarthy's next book. Published in 1968, it is far more disturbing and pessimistic than his debut, and yet also more steeped in a sense of God and absence. The novel's title appears to be a reference to the Matthean concept of outer darkness, some place of "weeping and gnashing of teeth" that is not quite Hell, but close.

Also set in a version of east Tennessee, *Outer Dark* is the story of Culla Holme and his sister, Rinthy, whom he has impregnated. McCarthy begins the book with a dislocated prologue: a trio of mysterious figures, "their shadows long on the sawgrass and burnt sedge."[14] They rest at a river before moving further along their journey.

They are not the only wanderers in the book. The tinker, a collector and barter of trinkets, is introduced like some wood nymph, "a small gnomic creature wreathed in a morass of grizzled hair, watching him with bland gray eyes."[15] He visits the

Holmes, and three days after his arrival, Rinthy feels a "spasm in her belly."[16] She has the baby in the cabin, but Culla takes the child away into the night. The ethereal wilderness of *The Orchard Keeper* is replaced by the ominous feel of *Outer Dark*, in which the "sand of the road was scored and banded with shadow, dark beneath the pine and cedar trees or fiddlebacked with the slender shade of cane. Shadows which kept compass against all the road's turnings. He stopped from time to time, holding the child gingerly, listening."[17]

Culla takes the child deeper into the woods. He runs through a creek and then falls to the ground. In the distance, a "crack of lightning went bluely down the sky."[18] Unable to love the baby, he ditches the child in the forest. The tinker discovers the baby "in a cup of moss, naked and crying no louder than a kitten."[19] The tinker brings the boy into town, and gets a woman to take care of him. Meanwhile, Culla lies to his sister, frantic over the missing child. She wants to know where it is buried; she wants to give it a name. "It's dead," Culla tells her. "You don't name things dead," introducing a theme that will return in several of McCarthy's novels: the sense that an unnamed soul is an unbaptized and unsaved one (the belief that unbaptized children would go to purgatory, while never Catholic dogma, was a fear of Catholics for many years, certainly during the years of McCarthy's own faith).[20]

Rinthy rejects her brother's claims, and heads out to look for her child, "her bouquet clutched in both hands before her she stepped finally into the clearing, a swatch of grass, sunlight, birdcalls, crossing with quiet and guileless rectitude to stand before a patch of black and cloven earth."[21] She is McCarthy's first developed female character, a perversion of a Marian figure out to save her suffering son. She longs for him, and McCarthy writes with gentle yet funereal gestures: "A cool wind came out of the forest.

From time to time she stopped and listened but there was nothing to hear. She heard her steps small and faint in the silence. When she saw the light through the trees before her she stopped again, warily, her hands to her labored heart."[22] From his first to most recent books, McCarthy regularly includes characters who not only operate on the fringe of society, but appear to be vestiges of an earlier form of man. His killers are ruthless, merciless, supernatural. Yet they walk in this world among those, like Rinthy, who struggle toward the light.

It is a profoundly Catholic vision, although it might not seem like one at first glance. At Knoxville Catholic, and at Immaculate Conception, McCarthy would have learned that evil is present in this world. That the devil walks among us, and that no modern, human-made method can save us. McCarthy's Catholic vision is not to be understood as one of sound Catholic theology in the sense that he is doctrinaire. Rather, McCarthy's vision contains an idiosyncratic Catholic sense; a mixture of his personal views of good and evil, along with the undeniably powerful storytelling of his family, his church, and his schooling.

"There's no such thing as life without bloodshed," McCarthy has pronounced, and that is not a merely sadistic vision.[23] In fact, whether or not he was doing so explicitly, McCarthy was affirming a Catholic sense of evil. In the Catholic view, evil is not to be understood. As St. Augustine lamented, "I sought whence evil comes and there was no solution." The Catholic tradition teaches that our prideful attempts to examine and conquer evil from an intellectual stance are folly. Christ alone is the only salvation from evil.

Critic Bryan Giemza has perceptively described McCarthy as a heretical Catholic—a writer whose framework is Catholic, but whose nightmarish visions rarely offer salvation. Rinthy doesn't find what she is looking for, literally, or spiritually. Her breasts teem with milk, confounding the town doctor, who says "No woman carries milk six months for a dead baby."[24] She rejects him, saying her milk proves the child is still alive. She is right, but the child is not safe. The tinker still has the baby, and McCarthy describes them both as if they exist outside this world: "*What discordant vespers do the tinker's goods chime through the long twilight and over the brindled forest road, him stooped and hounded through the windy recrements of day like those old exiles who divorced of corporeality and enjoined ingress of heaven or hell wander forever the middle warrens spoorless increate and anathema.*"[25]

The tinker sets the child in front of a fire to sleep, but the three mysterious men arrive. By the time Culla finds them, the tinker is dead, hung from a tree. Culla spots the worn and weary child, stuck in the dust in front of the unholy trinity of men. "What are you?" Culla asks them, as if he considers them ghosts, not humans.[26] He picks up the child, and it dangles from his hands "like a dressed rabbit, a gross eldritch doll with ricketsprung legs and one eye opening and closing softly like a naked owl's."[27] He doesn't seem to love the boy. He says the child "ain't nothin to me," and speaks with the men about how the child doesn't have a name.[28] One of the men tells Culla that "people in hell ain't got names."[29]

Culla isn't there to save the child; he is there to witness it. His half-hearted desire to return the baby to his sister isn't enough. One of the men picks up the child and slits its neck, and gives it to the mute who "buried his moaning face in its throat."[30] It is a vile scene, made more so because Culla doesn't try to stop them.

Later, Rinthy reaches the abandoned burial place, and "stepping softly with her air of blooded ruin about the glade in a frail agony of grace she trailed her rags through dust and ashes, circling the dead fire, the charred billets and chalk bones, the little calcined ribcage."[31] Vultures feed on the tinker's corpse, and as the seasons pass, his bones drop to the ground. There is no beauty, and no grace, in McCarthy's Godless world. Salvation never happened here. *Outer Dark* and other novels from this first period are full of sloppy, slovenly characters, as if to say—are these also children of God?

That question continues in the expansive *Suttree* (1979), a novel that McCarthy had been working on for years, and, if we are to believe his childhood friends, a book that he had been writing his entire life. *Suttree* is a pivot in McCarthy's canon. The novel is a paean to midcentury Knoxville, a quirky, rollicking tale. Cornelius Suttree leaves his wealthy family to live as a fisherman on the Tennessee River. As a whole, the book is more comedic, optimistic, and conventional than his previous novels, although it carries forms of McCarthy's stylistic touches. *Suttree* dramatizes the strained Catholic paradox of parochial identity—the simultaneous rejection of clericalism and authority, and the pull toward the rituals and rhythms of faith.

Suttree's twin died during childbirth. "I followed him," Suttree describes, "to the world. . . . And used to pray for his soul days past. Believing this ghastly circus reconvened elsewhere for alltime. He in the limbo of the Christless righteous, I in a terrestrial hell."[32] His description of the traditional Augustinian and Thomist teaching that unbaptized children resided in purgatory is accurate to mid-twentieth-century Catholic thought, but also establishes an anti-Catholic verve to the novel, notably coming from Suttree himself.

His twin died unnamed, a continuation of a theme established in *Outer Dark*, as the unbaptized seem to pass through this world without document. Without his twin, Suttree drifts around Knoxville on a spiritual search. He walks through town one night and sees a black congregation led by a "preacher that looked like a storybook blackbird in his suit and goldwire spectacles."[33] He listens to their gospel songs. "He has watched them summer nights, a pale pagan. . . . He has stayed in a peace that drained his mind, for even a false admiration of the world of the spirit is better than none at all."[34] A lapsed Catholic, Suttree is often drawn to street preachers and pontificators as a more accurate representation of God than institutional Christianity. He moved "among vendors and beggars and wild street preachers haranguing a lost world with a vigor unknown to the sane. Suttree admired them with their hot eyes and dogeared bibles, God's barkers gone forth into the world like the prophets of old. He'd often stood among the edges of the crowd for some stray scrap of news from beyond the pale."[35]

Suttree describes himself as a "defrocked" Catholic.[36] The leader of an evangelical group that Suttree encounters asks if he has been saved, and Suttree says he's only been baptized "on the head," to which the old man responds "That old sprinklin business wont get it, buddy boy."[37] Suttree's Catholicism is portrayed as distinctly not American, an oddity in Knoxville. Despite his lack of practice and outward faith, Suttree's Catholicism is his unique trait, particularly during solemn moments. When one Protestant character is about to drop his dead father's body into the river, he asks Suttree to say some words of ritual, to which he responds, "The only words I know are the Catholic ones."[38]

After that scene, Suttree, drunk, shows up at the Church of the Immaculate Conception, the church of his youth. "The virtues of a stainless birth were not lost on him, no not on him," he thinks, as he enters the church "and paused by a concrete seashell filled with sacred waters. He stood in the open door. He entered."[39] Suttree sits in the front pew and describes the kneelers as places "where rows of hemorroidal dwarfs convene by night."[40]

He looks around and sees "a sallow plaster Christ. Agonized beneath his muricate crown. Spiked palms and riven belly, there beneath the stark ribs the cleanlipped spear-wound. His caved haunches loosely girdled, feet crossed and fastened by a single nail. To the left his mother. Mater alchimia in skyblue robes, she treads a snake with her chipped and naked feet."[41] McCarthy's mixture of Latin language and rhythm with English creates a syntax in the tradition of Joyce's *Ulysses*, another novel whose Catholic character blends sarcasm with the sacred.

Suttree thinks of his past spent in the church: "Like the child that sat in these selfsame bones so many black Fridays in terror of his sins. Viceridden child, heart rotten with fear. Listening to the slide shoot back in the confessional, waiting his turn."[42] He moves on to a more pleasant memory of May processions, the Catholic devotion to the Virgin Mary that occurs on the final day of that month. McCarthy would have participated in that Marian procession himself during his twelve years of Catholic schooling. "The stained-glass saints lay broken in their panes of light among the pews and in the summer afternoon quietude a smell of old varnish and the distant cries of children in a playground," Suttree thinks.[43] He remembers the movements of the priest, the "censer swings in chains, clinks back and forth, at the apex of each arc coughing up a quick gout of smoke. The priest dips the aspergillum in a gold bucket. He casts left and right, holy water upon the congregation."[44]

He snaps out of his sentimental reverie as he remembers seeing "two scullery nuns stand bowed in fouled habits" and his service as an altar boy, those hours "proscribed and doom in store, doom's adumbration in the smoky censer, the faint creak of the tabernacle door, the tasteless bread and draining the last of the wine from the cruet in a corner and counting the money in the box."[45]

Suttree's distaste for the Catholic faith seems to be rooted in a rejection of the priesthood. Although he finds nostalgic beauty in the rituals, Suttree derides the priests as "grim and tireless in their orthopedic moralizing. Filled with tales of sin and unrepentant deaths and visions of hell and stories of levitation and possession and dogmas of semitic damnation for the tacking up of the paraclete."[46] That feeling continues to the present; when Suttree falls asleep in the church, he is awakened by a priest with a "bland scented face."[47] The priest gently reprimands him for sleeping, and Suttree says "It's not God's house," repeating it twice.[48]

It seems like young Charlie McCarthy was much politer during his own parochial years. Suttree's rejection of the church comes from his desire to affirm his self as separate from all forms of patriarchy: father, country, and institution. Late in the novel, during a "clear night over south Knoxville," Suttree talks to himself: "Tilting back in his chair he framed questions for the quaking ovoid of lamplight on the ceiling to pose to him."[49] He asks himself if it is true that "the last shall be first," and clarifies that he believes "that the last and the first suffer equally."[50]

Ravaged with typhoid fever near the novel's conclusion, Suttree's hallucinations are interrupted by a priest who has arrived to administer the Last Rites. He hears the priest's "maudlin voice chant latin by his bedside, what medieval ghost come to usurp his fallen corporeality. An oiled thumball redolent of lime and sage pondered his shuttered lids."[51] The priest's "lamptanned and angular face leaned over him. The room was candlelit and spiced with smoke. He closed his eyes. A cool thumb crossed his soles with unction."[52]

It is only appropriate that when the priest returns another morning, he has a playful banter with the ailing Suttree. When the priest asks if Suttree wishes to confess, he responds "I did it."[53]

Suttree, living a purgatorial existence along the river, is a Catholic trickster—a Joycean vision in Knoxville. *Suttree* is McCarthy's most comic novel, and a unique document of midcentury American Catholic anxiety: the skepticism of a clerical world that would change with the coming advent of Vatican II. That McCarthy chose to capture this particular time period suggests that his Catholic sense is firmly in those days of Latin Mass.

Although McCarthy worked on *Suttree* for years while living in Tennessee—at one point living in a dairy barn near Knoxville and bathing in a lake because he refused opportunities to speak and read from his books—the novel was published while he was living in El Paso, Texas. In December 1981, he learned that he was awarded a generous grant from the MacArthur Foundation. He bought a small home in El Paso, and has since never left the Southwest—its landscape, people, and mythos leading to his most prolific, and popular, literary output.

Blood Meridian, his next novel, was published in 1985, and is his first book to contain epigraphs, including one from Lutheran theologian Jacob Boehme's 1620 treatise, *Six Theosophic Points*: "It is not to be thought that the life of darkness is sunk in misery and lost as if in sorrowing. There is no sorrowing. For sorrow is a thing that is swallowed up in death, and death and dying are the very life of the darkness." The novel's opening line—"See the child"— evokes the cadence of both Herman Melville and the Bible.[54] The boy is described in mythic terms: "He can neither read nor write and in him broods already a taste for mindless violence. All history present in that visage, the child the father of the man."[55]

At fourteen years old, he runs away from home, and soon leaves Tennessee. The boy crosses the country, and in 1849 he arrives in Nacogdoches, Texas, on the back of an old mule. In the first scene of the novel's present storyline, a reverend preaches to a standing-room crowd in a tent. Rain slaps the canvas as he gives a sermon. He is interrupted by a mysterious man who parts the crowd, and then addresses them from the preacher's own crate-board pulpit. The man claims the reverend is a false prophet, and soon gunfire rages among the congregants. They knife the tent into shreds and trample each other in the mud.

The mysterious man is Judge Holden, and later, at a bar with the kid and others, he admits that he's never seen the preacher before that day—he just wanted to cause trouble. His action introduces the dark comedy that suffuses *Blood Meridian*, a comedy that is far more sinister than the playfulness of *Suttree*. It is best to think of *Blood Meridian* along the wavelength of *Outer Dark*—full of character-spirits whose madness and menace feel devilish.

McCarthy cultivates their myth through his grand descriptions of characters in transit: "Days of riding where there rode no soul save he. He's left behind the pinewood country and the evening sun declines before him beyond an endless swale and dark falls here like a thunderclap and a cold wind sets the weeds to gnash-ing."[56] In one scene, the kid awakens in an abandoned church on the floor "deep in dried guano and the droppings of cattle and sheep. Pigeons flapped through the piers of dusty light and three buzzards hobbled about on the picked bone carcass of some animal dead in the chancel."[57] Cracked and crushed, the church itself is a testament to a defaced belief: "The facade of the building bore an array of saints in their niches and they had been shot up by American troops trying their rifles, the figures shorn of ears and noses and darkly mottled with leadmarks oxidized upon the stone. The huge carved and paneled doors hung awap on their hinges and a carved stone Virgin held in her arms a headless child."[58]

The kid is recruited to join an army who seek to reclaim Mexican land, and once they reach there, McCarthy describes another church as a gateway to the past. "Long buttresses of light fell from the high windows in the western wall. There were no pews in the church and the stone floor was heaped with the scalped and naked and partly eaten bodies of some forty souls who'd barricaded themselves in this house of God against the heathen."[59] The faithful had been slaughtered in the church, and their "primitive painted saints in their frames hung cocked on the walls as if an earthquake had visited and a dead Christ in a glass bier lay broken in the chancel floor."[60]

Banished to a Mexican prison, the kid again encounters the Judge and meets a scalp hunter who leads the Glanton Gang, a group who hunts Indians at the Texas-Mexico border. McCarthy's depiction is loosely based on John Joel Glanton, but whatever historical precedent established is blurred by his penchant for making his characters feel ancient and apocalyptic. The gang seems like a cult of spirits: "They rode like men invested with a purpose whose origins were antecedent to them, like blood legatees of an order both imperative and remote."[61]

Blood Meridian, with its violence and heretical images, is a noteworthy book in McCarthy's sequence of novels that appear to depict an earthly Hell. After leaving Chihuahua, the gang reaches a town in a gorge named Jesús María where, after the morning rain stops, the men "appeared in the streets, tattered, stinking, ornamented with human parts like cannibals."[62] Whether they move along streets, rivers, or creeks, McCarthy's characters often engage in linear processions—a distinctly Catholic public ceremony of ardent faith, yet subverted by the actions of unbelievers. At night, a heretical clan of "besotted bedlamites lurching and cursing and ringing the churchbells with pistolballs in a godless charivari" are reprimanded by a crucifix-bearing priest who exhorts "them with fragments of latin in a singsong chant."[63]

The clan harasses him, throwing rocks and mocking him as the priest "lay clutching his image" of Christ.[64]

In another scene of surreal Catholic spectacle, a priest "ringing a small bell" leads a procession that includes a makeshift Christ, "a poor figure of straw with carven head and feet. He wore a crown of mountain briars and on his brow were painted drops of blood and on his old dry wooden cheeks blue tears. The villagers knelt and blessed themselves and some stepped forward and touched the garment the figure wore and kissed their fingertips."[65] McCarthy often returns to such hallucinatory, public moments of piety.

Tobin, one of the men in the kid's marauding group, is often referred to as "expriest," although he clarifies that he was not a priest but a Jesuit novitiate. During a pause in the novel's violence, the Judge talks about morality. "Moral law," he claims, "is an invention of mankind for the disenfranchisement of the powerful in favor of the weak."[66] He asks what Tobin thinks, but Tobin doesn't answer. The Judge mocks him, using his Latin: "The priest does not say . . . Nihil dicit. But the priest has said. For the priest has put by the robes of his craft and taken up the tools of that higher calling which all men honor. The priest also would be a godserver but a god himself."[67]

Tobin tells the Judge that he has a "blasphemous tongue,"[68] and later in the novel Tobin stumbles "among the bones and holding aloft a cross he'd fashioned out of the shins of a ram and he'd lashed them together with strips of hide and he was holding the thing before him like some mad dowser in the bleak of desert and calling out in a tongue both alien and extinct."[69] Although terribly compromised, Tobin appears to be the religiously moral witness to the Judge's depravity. *Blood Meridian*'s overwhelming violence is somewhere between hallucination and parody—or perhaps it is both. In portraying a world without God, where even

His churches are broken and graffitied, McCarthy suggests that violence and despair reigns in a world that longs for an absent God.

What characters might do to receive grace in such a world is an essential question of McCarthy's work. Despite the wavering and even absent faith of his characters, they live against an architecture of Christian tradition in which sin, despair, and evil are not intellectual constructs, but as literal as their own flesh and blood. McCarthy's disinterest in salvation does not lessen his Christian vision. The world he presents is incomplete and broken—one in need of a second coming.

The Road, McCarthy's most recent novel, is a dramatic investigation of how we envision God amidst destruction. Unlike the metaphorically apocalyptic scenes of earlier novels, *The Road* depicts an actual cataclysmic event. McCarthy has admitted that the book is a love story: the absolute devotion of parent to child.

The book is dedicated to his youngest son, John, born in 1998. The tale of father and son opens with the line, "When he woke in the woods in the dark and the cold of the night he'd reach out to touch the child sleeping beside him."[70] In this decimated world, bands of marauders savage the scant population for food. The unnamed father and son roam in secret, only hoping to survive.

When the son asks the father what he would do if the child died, the father responds, "If you died I would want to die too. . . . So I could be with you."[71] *The Road* is McCarthy's most desolate novel, but it is also full of love. The family's mother, wracked with despair, killed herself, and her absence implores the father and son to keep moving. They want to be with her again.

In the meanwhile, the characters find some comfort in ritual. The boy sleeps in front of a fire, and the father "tousled his hair before the fire to dry it. All of this like some ancient anointing.

So be it. Evoke the forms. Where you've nothing else construct ceremonies out of the air and breathe upon them."[72] Yet the father's strength wanes. "There were times when he sat watching the boy sleep that he would begin to sob uncontrollably but it wasnt about death. He wasnt sure what it was about but he thought it was about beauty or about goodness."[73]

Wounded from an arrow attack, the father dies in the final pages of the novel, but the boy is taken in by another family. "He tried to talk to God but the best thing was to talk to his father and he did talk to him and he didnt forget. The woman said that was all right. She said that the breath of God was his breath yet though it pass from man to man through all of time."[74] The father's ardent hope lives on in the boy.

In a 2012 interview with a television station in Spain, McCarthy was asked about *The Road*. He acknowledges that many readers think the book is dark and depressing, but he says it is purely about "the love between the father and the son." The book "attempts to show that love can survive even under the most horrible circumstances, and if you really love someone, if you really love your son, then it doesn't make any difference how bad the world gets, you'll stick with them and you'd die for them."

When asked once if he remained a Catholic, McCarthy said "I have a great sympathy for the spiritual view of life, and I think that it's meaningful. But am I a spiritual person? I would like to be. Not that I am thinking about some afterlife that I want to go to, but just in terms of being a better person."[75] Cormac McCarthy's fiction is concerned with life, death, and God. Even his domestic scenes carry the gravity of eternity—as if the mess of our daily lives exists on the continuum of tradition. In his 2017 essay "The Kekulé Problem," one of his rare works of nonfiction, McCarthy considers the power and mystery of language. Our human ability to communicate has been a blessing and burden. We are graced with the power of story—but how? McCarthy stops short of naming God as the source of that grace, but he is skeptical of a purely evolutionary conception of language.

He ends his essay with a series of questions about our unconscious. "What does it know about itself? Does it know that it's going to die? What does it think about that?"[76] McCarthy has no answers. He seems fine without them—in fiction, and in life.

7

TWO CULTURES,
TWO FAITHS

Louise Erdrich

There is a confessional—where penitents would once whisper their sins—in a Minneapolis, Minnesota bookstore. The center door has been removed. A lone bulb shines from the top, light reflecting off paper taped to the inside walls. On each side books sit on shelves. The confessional was set to become a sound booth at a bar, but it was saved, and decorated with sweetgrass rosaries. Salvation, it seems, can come in surprising forms.

Birchbark Books is not a Catholic bookstore, but it is owned by a Catholic: Louise Erdrich. The novelist converted the former meat market into an independent bookstore in 2001. In addition to her selection of books—with her own handwritten recommendations hanging from shelves—Erdrich also sells Native artwork, foods, and gifts. "One side is dedicated to Cleanliness," Erdrich writes on the bookstore's website, "the other to Godliness."[1] She jokes that she is "currently collaging the interior with images of her sins," but ensures that the confessional "is now a forgiveness booth, there for the dispensation of random absolution."[2]

Erdrich has spent a lifetime revising, rejecting, appreciating, parodying, and performing Catholicism. Her bookstore confessional is an extension of her fiction: comic and complex, faith out in the open. A prolific writer across several genres, Erdrich's writing consistently includes lay and clerical Catholics, nuns and sinners and blasphemers. Her work is so suffused with Catholicism that it brings to mind Flannery O'Connor. Erdrich says she loves her literary ancestor because "everything is so Catholic and bizarre at the same time" in O'Connor's fiction.[3] And yet, unlike O'Connor, Erdrich is not often identified as a Catholic writer. Out in plain sight, she remains mysterious as a writer of faith.

Erdrich is by turns hilarious, self-effacing, and introspective—inclined to spin yarns. Born in 1954 in Little Falls, Minnesota, she grew up in Wahpeton, North Dakota. Her mother was Chippewa; her father German American. Erdrich was taught by Franciscan Sisters, including a sixth-grade nun who "hit home runs at recess."[4] She would regularly visit family on the nearby Turtle Mountain Chippewa reservation, a land "missionized by Benedictine priests and by Benedictine nuns."[5] She describes her mother as "a very strong Catholic. Very wonderful, I think, in her level of faith and understanding."[6]

Erdrich's mother inherited that Catholic identity from her own father, Erdrich's maternal grandfather Patrick Gourneau. Perhaps more than any other family member, her grandfather demonstrated what would become the dualities and complexities of Erdrich's spiritual and cultural identities. He was tribal chairman of the Turtle Mountain Reservation, and practiced both Catholic and traditional Chippewa religions.

"Catholicism is very important up there at Turtle Mountain," Erdrich recalls. "When you go up there, you go to Church! My grandfather has had a real mixture of old time and church religion—which is another way of incorporating. He would do pipe ceremonies for ordinations and things like that. He just had a grasp on both realities, in both religions."[7] Erdrich says that her grandfather refused "to see distinctions between the embodiments of the spirit. He prayed in the woods, he prayed in the mission, to him it was all connected."[8]

Erdrich would follow him to the treeline of those woods and listen to his prayers, which were spoken in Ojibwe, a language that a young midcentury Catholic like Erdrich would think was "like Latin," a "ceremonial language."[9] Even the Turtle Mountain priests, Erdrich remembers, "were at the time amenable to a syncretic belief system."[10]

She always had eclectic tastes. While in high school, she was a cheerleader for the wrestling team, wore her father's National Guard clothing, listened to Joan Baez, and could be found "keeping journals and reading poems and trying to be a little different."[11] She continued writing poetry in college at Dartmouth, part of the first class containing women, and published her first poems as a senior in *Ms.* magazine and the *Carolina Quarterly*. After she graduated, more poems appeared in *Shenandoah*, *Louisville Review*, and other literary magazines. She entered the MA program in writing at Johns Hopkins and began writing and publishing fiction, including work in *Redbook* under the pseudonym Milou North.

Upon graduation from the Johns Hopkins program in 1980, Erdrich became communications director and editor of *The Circle*, a Native American newspaper. Although she had been writing and publishing poetry for several years, the experience changed her—and her subject matter. "Settling into that job and becoming comfortable with an urban community—which is very different from the reservation community—gave me another reference point," she said. "There were lots of people with mixed blood, lots of people who had their own confusions. I realized that this was part of my life—it wasn't something that I was making up—and that it was something I *wanted* to write about. I wanted to tell it because it was something that should be told."[12]

Her own "confusions" became thematic fodder for her fictional characters. Following publication of stories in *The Atlantic Monthly* and the *Best American Short Stories*, Erdrich released *Love Medicine*, her debut novel-in-stories, in 1984. The book contains interconnected chapters that all feel like discrete and complete short stories. Her prose is inventive—simultaneously playful and dark—and dramatizes an Ojibwe reservation much like Turtle Mountain. One particularly evocative story, "Saint Marie," is narrated by young Marie Lazarre, a Chippewa girl who decides that she is going to go "up there on the hill with the black robe women"—the nuns of the Sacred Heart convent.[13]

Marie wants to become a saint. She imagines becoming an icon "carved in pure gold. With ruby lips."[14] In contrast to her vision, the Sacred Heart convent is dilapidated, with "cracked whitewash and swallows nesting in the busted ends of eaves."[15] Fruit trees are bare, and goldenrod "rubbed up their walls."[16] Rumor had it that Sacred Heart "was a catchall place for nuns that don't get along elsewhere. Nuns that complain too much or lose their mind."[17] It was a place where "maps stopped," where "God had only half a mind in the creation. Where the Dark One had put in thick bush, liquor, wild dogs and Indians."[18]

Speaking of the devil: one Sister Leopolda had a special interest in the source of evil. She "kept track of him and knew his habits, minds he burrowed in, deep spaces where he hid."[19] The nun even had "a long oak pole for opening high windows" that she kept in the classroom, used "for catching Satan by surprise."[20]

Like Sister Leopolda, Marie is a believer that the devil is out and about. "Evil was a common thing I trusted," she says.[21] "Before sleep sometimes he came and whispered conversation in the old language of the bush. I listened. He told me things he never told anyone but Indians."[22] While Marie thinks her Native blood offers her preternatural gifts in recognizing evil, Sister Leopolda is skeptical of the new student. One day during class, Marie thinks the devil is hiding in the closets at the back of the room. She smirks during a lesson, and the nun notices. Sister Leopolda "grabbed me by the collar and dragged me, feet flying, through the room and threw me in the closet with her dead black overboot."[23]

To know the devil, the nun concludes, is to be devilish. She wants to drive the devil from Marie, and even soaks the girl's back with scalding water. Marie's own obsession with the nun grows. She thinks she could have any man that she wanted on the reservation, but she actually "wanted Sister Leopolda's heart. And here was the thing: sometimes I wanted her heart in love and admiration. Sometimes. And sometimes I wanted her heart to roast on a black stick."[24]

In a darkly comic scene that is classic Erdrich fare, Marie kicks the nun into a bread oven, but Leopolda's "outstretched poker hit the back wall first, so she rebounded."[25] Furious, the nun stabs Marie in the hand with the poker, but it only results in the other sisters of Sacred Heart becoming convinced that Marie has the stigmata. Leopolda wants them to think this so that she doesn't have to acknowledge the attack, but it makes Marie into a saint—the power she always wanted.

Marie's ambition in *Love Medicine* curiously reflects Erdrich's own youth. When asked during a PBS interview if she had wanted to become a priest while growing up, she said yes: "I wanted the power of the priest. The priest had a great deal of power. And I think a lot of the women who taught me who were Franciscan sisters could have been happier as priests. Their power was thwarted."[26] Her representation of Catholic nuns is playful but not wholly parodic; she perceives them as a feminine source of power and tension in the church.

Her fascination with the priesthood is at the center of her 2001 novel, *The Last Report on the Miracles at Little No Horse*. Set in North Dakota, the novel is told in achronological chapters, and begins in 1996. Father Damien Modeste, now an old man, sits "in his favorite chair, contemplating the graveyard that spread just past the ragged yard behind his retirement house and up a low hill."[27] Although slowed down by age, "he still excelled at listening to confessions"—he "enjoyed hearing sins, chewing other people's stories, and then with a flourish absolving and erasing their wrongs, sending sinners out of the church clean and new."[28]

At the end of the first chapter we see his nightly routine, which happens no matter how exhausted he feels: "He lifted a neatly folded nightshirt from the top dresser drawer and laid it on the bed. Then, with slow care, he turned off the bedside lamps and in moonlighted dark unwound from his chest a wide Ace bandage. His woman's breasts were small, withered, modest as folded flowers. He slipped his nightshirt over his head and took a deep breath of relief before crawling between the covers."[29]

After this revelation, the novel rewinds to around 1910, when a woman named Agnes DeWitt has taken the identity of Sister Cecilia: "shorn, houseled, clothed in black wool and bound in starched linen of heatless white."[30] She taught and played music, the piano, where "she existed in her essence, a manifestation of compelling sound."[31] Her piano playing moves from the sensual to the erotic, and becomes a distraction at the convent. The Mother Superior implores her to change her songs. Afterward, "life in the convent returned to normal."[32] The "floors stopped groaning and absorbed fresh wax. The doors ceased to fly open for no reason and closed discreetly. The water stopped rushing continually through the pipes as the sisters no longer took advantage of the new plumbing to drown out the sounds of their emotions."[33]

Full of a passion that she cannot control, Agnes flees the convent, and marries, but is soon widowed when her husband is killed by a bank robber. Depressed, she is unable to leave her home. A priest who has been assigned to "missionize Indians" arrives at her home, offering her communion.[34]

The priest never reaches the mission—he drowns during a flood, his body stuck on a branch after a car accident. Agnes wraps him in her nightgown, puts on his vestments, and buries his body. She then follows his route to the Ojibwe reservation that was to be his destination.

The swiftness of Agnes's actions and transformation are made authentic by Erdrich's narrative skill. What could be a convoluted story for other writers feels natural for Erdrich. Agnes, now Father Damien, is reborn, and her arrival at the Little No Horse reservation is wonderfully lyric: "There was stillness, the whisper of snow grains driven along the surface of the world. It was the silence of before creation, the comfort of pure nothing, and she let herself go into it until, in that quiet, she was caught hold of by a dazzling sweetness."[35]

Inside the "crooked-built church," Father Damien finds six nuns saying their morning prayers: "They knelt, hunched in cold, swathed in layers of patched wool, quiet as stones."[36]

She celebrates her first Mass there, and feels a "panic of emotion" while giving the Eucharist to the nuns.[37] It is her first experience of priestly ecstasy, and she feels enraptured by it. She wonders if the nuns were physically sustained—not simply spiritually nourished—by the Host.

Father Damien soon discovers the dual identity of many people she encounters on the reservation. One man's deftness with the English language came from his Jesuit schooling, but the man "had stubbornly retained and deepened his Ojibwemowin" and would write and think in that language.[38] Despite the complexities of ministering as an outsider, Agnes settles into her role as Father Damien.

The faith of those at Little No Horse is strong. The Feast of the Virgin is described in brimming detail: "The day continued mild and glorious, and as the sun's light strengthened the Catholics fell in line behind the cart bearing a borrowed statue, for the parish hadn't one of its own yet. As they passed along, men fell to their knees in the dust of the road and women raised a trill—a high-pitched tongue of wild joy."[39]

Father Damien's own faith is also strong, but stressed. She prays four times a day: when she wakes, at noon, late afternoon, and before she went to bed. Yet her "struggle with the Ojibwe language, the influence of it, had an effect on her prayers. For she preferred the Ojibwe word for praying, anama'ay, with its sense of a great motion upward. She began to address the trinity as four and to include the spirit of each direction—those who sat at the four corners of the earth."[40]

Erdrich has spoken about the importance of the number 4, which is "the number of completion in Ojibway mythology. There are different myths, but one of them is the bear coming through different worlds, breaking through from one world into the next, from the next world into the next world. The number of incompletion is three and the number of completion is four, so four is a *good* number."[41]

Despite her attempts to become part of the culture at Little No Horse, Father Damien often feels overwhelmed. Once, while sick, she writes the bishop in exasperation, and his solution is to send an assistant priest, Father Gregory Wekkle, to the parish. Agnes is immediately attracted to him. They quickly become close, and in a twist that feels inevitable but still shocking, they have sex. He wants to get married, but she won't. Agnes affirms her transformed identity: "I am a priest."[42]

Yet she is torn once he leaves: "Awful questions appeared in Agnes's mind. Am I right? Can I bear this? Have I invented my God? Is God my yearning? Is my yearning God?"[43] Her literal and metaphysical crises fracture her identity. Depressed, she spends long hours asleep, spent "wandering mightily through heaven and earth," her mind "exploring worlds inhabited by both Ojibwe and Catholic."[44]

She soon starts playing the piano again, and a "grand wave of baptisms followed" in response to the music.[45] She remains fraught by nagging questions: "Had the devil in its original tempter's form returned her art, or had God? And furthermore, what did it matter?"[46] Erdrich's characters waver between faith and doubt, and between Ojibwe and Catholic beliefs—implying that rather than being mutually exclusive, these faiths can both complement and contrast each other. The tandem existence of both beliefs only adds to the mystery of God within her fiction.

Erdrich continues to examine the ambiguity between Ojibwe and Catholic beliefs in her 2012 novel, *The Round House*, which begins with the rape of a woman, Geraldine Coutts, on a North Dakota reservation. Narrated by her teenage son Joe, the novel considers how trauma is personal, familial, and spiritual—the rape occurs near the round house, which had long been used for traditional Native ceremonies. The townspeople would bring their Bibles to the round house and pretend it was a dance hall; once they saw the parish priest approaching down the road, they would rush to clean up. Before the priest arrived, "the water drums and eagle feathers and the medicine bags and birchbark scrolls and sacred pipes were in a couple of motorboats halfway across the lake. The Bible was out and people were reading aloud from Ecclesiastes."[47]

After the attack, Geraldine and her husband Bazil start sleeping in different rooms. A friend asks Bazil if it would help if Geraldine went to church. He doesn't think his wife would find comfort there. She'd stopping going to church after Catholic boarding school. But there's a new priest, Father Travis Wozniak, a Benedictine from Dallas, Texas, and a former Marine. One character says "He gives very questioning sermons. . . . Sometimes I wonder if he's entirely stable, or then again, if he might be simply . . . intelligent."[48] He taught catechism class "like Vatican II had never happened . . . [and] said Latin mass if he felt like it and for several months the previous winter had turned the altar away from the congregation and conducted the Mysteries with a sort of wizardly flourish."[49]

He also, at least initially, appears to be a suspect in the crime. The young narrator and his friend Angus become unlikely investigators. They go to Mass at Sacred Heart to spy on the priest, but sneak out during Holy Communion, and go to the playground to smoke. After Mass, Father Travis comes outside and reprimands them, but also seems a bit eerie. The narrator says the "sheen off his cassock reflecting up into his eyes spooked me."[50] Their curiosity piqued further; the boys decide to spy on the priest in his rectory—they see him watch *Alien*, as well as undress and change.

Later, long after the priest is pronounced innocent, Joe attends a Youth Encounter Camp: "We caught hands all around and put our heads down and prayed the Hail Mary, which you don't have to be a Catholic to know on this reservation as people mutter it at all hours in the grocery store or bars or school hallways."[51] Even Joe is aware that Catholicism and reservation life have become inseparable: "Priests and nuns have been here since the beginning of the reservation. Even the most traditional Indians, the people who'd kept the old ceremonies alive in secret, either had Catholicism beaten into them in boarding school, or had made friends with some of the more interesting priests . . . or they had decided to hedge their bets by adding the saints to their love of the sacred pipe."[52]

Erdrich, perhaps more so than any other contemporary American fiction writer, demonstrates the collision between Catholicism and ethnicity. Although writers like Don DeLillo capture the complexity of the American Catholic immigrant experience, his characters carry their Catholic faith across oceans and generations. Even Toni Morrison, whose own personal Catholicism sometimes collided with the black Protestant traditions of her fictions, does not consistently center Catholic faith and identity in her novels. It is not possible to read Louise Erdrich without simultaneously living within a Catholic milieu; again and again, the central fount and tension of that world is the duel identities of Catholic and Ojibwe life.

In *LaRose*, her 2016 novel, Erdrich tells the tragic tale of Landreaux Iron, "a devout Catholic who also followed traditional ways, a man who would kill a deer, thank one god in English, and put down tobacco for another god in Ojibwe."[53] The novel begins with Landreaux hunting for deer. He tries to shoot a buck, but accidently kills his neighbor's five-year-old son, Dusty Ravich. The death shatters both families.

Father Travis Wozniak returns in this novel and is more fully and closely developed as a character. He'd "long ago stopped giving sermons. He just told stories."[54] During one Mass he "walked out into the middle of the aisle and acted out the meeting between Saint Francis and the wolf."[55]

Landreaux's wife, Emmaline, goes to the priest for help and counsel. He is praying the rosary while she speaks to him. At 46, he'd returned to his Marine ways, but was "powerful, deeper, sadder."[56] A slightly comic character in her previous work, the priest is now a leader: "In his life on the reservation, Father Travis had seen how some people would try their best but the worst would still happen."[57]

The Iron and Ravich families need a leader—a guide. Landreaux and Emmaline make a life-changing decision: they give their son, LaRose, to the grieving family. The gift of a child in such circumstances was a community tradition, but that does not make the decision anything short of haunting. The name LaRose "was a name both innocent and powerful, and had belonged to the family's healers. . . . There had been a LaRose in each generation of Emmaline's family for over a hundred years."[58]

When LaRose randomly sees his mother in the grocery store, he runs to her and "they melted together."[59] Emmaline is distraught and can't go home. Instead, she "was drawn to the church. She then thought that she might pray there, for peace. But instead she walked around back of the church."[60] She walks with Father Travis along a fitness trail he'd built in the woods. She tells him that she didn't want to give LaRose to the family. "I want him back," she says.[61]

"Mary gave her child to the world," Father Travis also says, but then he quotes a version of Romans to her: *"Neither life, nor angels, nor principalities nor things present, nor things to come, nor powers, not height, nor depth, nor any other creature will separate you.*[62] She is not convinced. He realizes that he was being foolish in the moment—acting like a theologian when he should have been a counselor. He reminds her that, legally, her family can get back LaRose at any time.

Meanwhile, a new bishop is set to be named. Father Travis is nervous about what will happen and doesn't want another priest sent to the parish. He goes outside into the snow, and, "filled with an odd joy," thinks of the beauty of Midnight Mass on Christmas Eve.[63] He also thinks of Emmaline. His feelings for her are strong. The community "trusted him," he laments, "to be all things except, actually, human."[64]

He tells Emmaline that he's going to be transferred, and she begins to cry. She says to him: "You've always been here and you've done so much. Priests blow through here, but you've stayed. People love you."[65] He then tells her that he's fallen in love with her. She responds: "That's not fair."[66] She is speaking of love and lust; of what is acceptable and what is forbidden. Yet Emmaline captures what causes pain to so many of Erdrich's characters: the feeling that they must choose between heart and mind, between two identities that feel equally central to their being.

Future Home of the Living God, Erdrich's latest novel, unfolds that struggle against a dystopian backdrop. Structurally, the novel is an extended letter-diary from a woman to her child. Her name is Cedar Hawk Songmaker, but that is her "white name" as the "adopted child of Minneapolis liberals."[67] Her real Ojibwe name is Mary Potts.

She had an abortion a decade earlier. "In doing so," she writes to her child, "I opened a different door. If I hadn't had an abortion then, I would not be having *you,* now."[68] Her child is due on December 25th.

Cedar converted to Catholicism "first as a form of rebellion," but also because "I wanted an extended family—a whole parish of friends."[69] She's since become devout: "I have integrated both my ethnicity and my intellectual leanings into my faith first by analyzing the canonization of the Lily of the Mohawks, Kateri Tekakwitha, and then by editing, writing, illustrating, publishing, and distributing a magazine of Catholic inquiry called *Zeal*."[70] She writes the church newsletter. Her church, Holy Incarnation, "is a humble place—no limestone cathedral, no basilica."[71] The church "was founded to care for the most destitute people in the city, the cast-asides, the no-goods, the impossible, the toxic and contaminated."[72] It is "not a church of the saved, but a church of the lost."[73]

She became Catholic before meeting her biological mother, who is also Catholic. "Catholicism drew me," Cedar explains, "and I was fascinated by it all: the saints, the liturgy, even the little shrines. Now it turns out that the saints and the church are things we have in common."[74] Cedar's character upends the theme of missionizing Catholicism that exists in many of Erdrich's other novels; for Cedar, Catholic faith is her destiny and obsession. Reflecting on the drafting of the book, Erdrich explains she "had to cut hundreds of pages of Catholic inquiry."[75]

On her way to meet her biological mother for the first time, Cedar passes church billboards in fields, and in a "bare field, fallow and weedy, stretching to the pale horizon," one reads "*Future Home of the Living God*."[76] During the drive, she playfully ponders if "Perhaps all of creation from the coddling moth to the elephant was just a grandly detailed thought that God was engrossed in elaborating upon, when suddenly God fell asleep. We are an idea, then. Maybe God has decided that we are an idea not worth thinking anymore."[77]

Cedar's mother and fellow parishioners have built a shrine "on the reservation where people swear they have seen an apparition three times in the past four years."[78] They think it might be Kateri—the first Native American to be named a saint. "Again," Cedar writes to her future child, "here's that congruence. Catholic stuff."[79]

She accompanies her mother to the shrine, where a woman first says a prayer in Ojibwe. Cedar's mother, calling herself a "pagan Catholic," then tells the crowd Kateri's life story.[80] Afterward, she shares "financial impact statements from a site that has registered several appearances by the Virgin Mary" to demonstrate "what an effect pilgrimage crowds have on the local business community."[81] The group is folksy and silly about the event, but also steeped in real Marian devotion. In Erdrich's Catholic world, both coexist.

Erdrich seamlessly shifts from humor to solemnity; from the campy moments of religion to faith's most personal feelings. Her writing in the novel is at its most lyric when Cedar directly addresses her child within the letters: "I have already felt you move. Your bones are hardening, your brain is hooked up to stereo—your ears. So you can hear me, you can hear my voice. You can hear my praying in the car and as I enter the house. You can hear me as I read aloud the first words of my letter to you. I am going to tell you everything, bit by bit, day by day."[82]

Cedar identifies a contradiction in her faiths and identities, "the searcher who believes equally in the laws of physics and the Holy Ghost, in reading my favorite theologian, Hans Kung . . . and trying to live by the seven Ojibwe teachings, Truth Respect Love Bravery Generosity Wisdom Humility, which I've only read about and do not know from, say, a real Ojibwe person."[83] She is reading "The Madonna's Conception Through the Ear," a 1914 essay by psychoanalyst Ernest Jones, which is "an examination of the belief that

God's whispered breath caused the Incarnation"—Christ as God made flesh.[84] Cedar is fascinated by the idea of "a word so uncanny, a word so powerful, a word actually so divine that its expression infuses a woman's body with a pregnancy of godly nature."[85] Catholicism is equal parts mystical and intellectual for Erdrich and her characters. Neither trait neuters the other; instead, the mystical and intellectual strands of faith nurture each other.

Cedar loves the idea that "there exists a language or perhaps a pre-language made up of words so unthinkably holy they cannot be said, much less known" and writes to her son that "Perhaps you will know how to speak this language. Perhaps it is a language that we have forgotten in our present form. Perhaps you are dreaming in this language right now."[86] She is working on her own essay. She thinks of a gnostic text, a particular line that she has memorized: *"For I am the first and the last. I am the honored one and the scorned one. I am the whore and the holy one. I am the wife and the virgin."*[87] She is "comforted by the voice—it is so ferociously modern . . . For here I am, maybe a walking contradiction, maybe two species in one body . . . an insecure Ojibwe, a fledgling Catholic."[88]

The second half of *Future Home of the Living God* develops the dystopian plot—pregnant women are herded to birthing centers, and Cedar's fetus is of particular interest. Birth rates are dwindling, first among animals, and then for humans. Her child is born on Christmas: "You stared at me, holding on with an implacable strength, and I looked into the soul of the world."[89] He is taken from her arms, but she never stops thinking of him, and knows that he will one day read her words—her story. It is a remarkably hopeful, life-affirming conclusion to a novel. The book's ending might be sentimental, but that is because everything about Cedar—her first person voice, her epistolary mode, and her Catholicism—cause her unbridled emotion.

"I guess I have my beefs about Catholicism," Erdrich has said. "Although you never change once you're raised a Catholic—you've got that. You've got that symbolism, that guilt, you've got the whole works and you can't really change that. That's easy to talk about because you have to exorcise it somehow. That's why there's a lot of Catholicism" in her books.[90] Although she "grew up with all the accepted truths" of Catholicism, she doesn't "have a central metaphor for my life. I only have chaos."[91] Could that chaos, ultimately, be faith itself? Erdrich has said "It depends upon how that is defined. If I take it to mean a person whose characters ask questions about their origins in space and time, well, yes, and of course someone is often bumping up against crucial church dogma. Life is religious, I think, and that includes writing."[92]

When a writer from *The Paris Review* visited Erdrich's home in 2010, the interview was conducted in "a small attic room pleasantly cluttered with photographs, artifacts, and many more Catholic and Ojibwe totems, including moccasins, shells, bells, dice, bitterroot, a bone breastplate, an abalone shell for burning sage, a turtle stool, a Huichol mask with a scorpion across its mouth and a double-headed eagle on its brow, and a small army of Virgin statuettes."[93] Her attic room is much like her fiction: eccentric in tone, and an amalgam of detail. "I do not have an assured faith," Erdrich has said. "I am full of doubt. But even those who doubt can practice a faith, and can pray, and can try to act out of a tradition of kindness and love. My own emphasis is on how religion helps in this world and not how it might improve our standing in the next."[94]

She further describes this doubt as a "continual questioning." Doubt, for Erdrich, is necessary to her faith, both Catholic and Ojibwe: "My job is to address the mystery. My job is to doubt. My job is to keep searching, keep looking."[95] "Everything," Erdrich concludes, "is part of this mystery."[96]

An inclusive, expansive, Catholic mystery—one that just might cause a bookseller to put a space of forgiveness in her store. "I kept writing because I grew up as a Catholic," Erdrich says. "And my—the one place you're allowed to be emotional and to really talk about yourself is in the confessional."[97] There is a safety in that darkness—where, looking outward without sight, we are forced to look inward.

8

LITERARY FAITH
IN A SECULAR AGE

One summer night in Long Island in the early 1960s, the sky
"a bright navy above the pitched roofs and the thick suburban
trees," Rick comes to "claim" Sheryl, his ex-girlfriend.[1] He stands
outside her house, his screams shattering the calm night, where "a
sprinkler shot weak sprays of water, white in the growing darkness.
Behind the idling motors of the boys' cars you could still hear the
collective gurgle of filters in backyard pools."[2]

That night, "It seemed the whole world was wailing."[3] Men
fight teenagers, leaping "on one another like obese, short-legged
children, sliding and falling, raising chains that seemed to crumble
backward onto their shoulders, moving bats and hoes and wide
rakes that seemed as unwieldly as trees."[4]

That night changed the neighborhood. Fathers now came out
of their homes at dark, some still wearing "squares of gauze taped
over their foreheads or pink Band-Aids wrapped tightly around

every knuckle of one hand."[5] At the edge of their lawns, by the curbs, they reenact blows given and received, "adding now the grace that had been missing from the original performance, the witty dialogue, the triumph."[6] These men were reborn. "They had fought wars and come home to love their wives and sire their children," and had "grown housebound and too cautious, as shy as infants."[7] Now, after that night, "they were ready to take up this new challenge, were ready to save us, their daughters, from the part of love that was painful and tragic and violent, from all that we had already, even then, set our hearts on."[8]

Alice McDermott's second novel, *That Night* (1987), arrives with a recursive structure, using that frenetic night in Long Island as an axis point, a genesis, a theme, a refrain. Her fiction so often creates the feeling that time is a tight circle; that our present is inextricable from our past. Whether she is writing about teenage love gone bad, or about generations of Irish Catholic families weathering disease, loss, and regret, McDermott's storytelling feels both arresting and melancholic.

McDermott, along with Phil Klay, are contemporary Catholic writers with active faiths. They offer a useful bookend to the start of *Longing for an Absent God*; like Flannery O'Connor, Walker Percy, and Andre Dubus, these practicing Catholic writers are celebrated by secular awards, publications, and audiences. Catholicism inhabits the fiction of these writers at the levels of plot, character, setting, and language. Their literary Catholicism is sincere, but their sincerity is not simple; McDermott and Klay create nuanced, complex portraits of contemporary American Catholic life.

For Pynchon, DeLillo, Morrison, and McCarthy, Catholic faith is a source of story and symbol, but their longing for an absent God comes from a sometimes-distant religious practice. For Erdrich, God's shape and purpose remains in flux; her stories document a lifelong search—perhaps a longing to understand God. McDermott and Klay represent a final mode: Catholics whose devotion capture the strength of a lived faith. Taken together, the works of these three types of contemporary Catholic fiction writers capture a richly diverse storytelling tradition with significant resonance. Taken specifically, McDermott and Klay reveal how literary faith looks in a secular age.

McDermott began publishing novels in the early 1980s, placing her well within the canon of post–Vatican II American novelists. She was born in 1953 in Brooklyn but raised on Long Island. She was baptized when she was two weeks old at Saint Catherine of Siena, in Saint Albans, Queens. She went to Catholic schools, including Saint Boniface School in Elmont, Long Island, and Sacred Heart Academy in Hempstead.

"We were Catholics as inevitably as we were ourselves," she said of her family.[9] For Irish Catholics like them, "Catholicism is there from the beginning of time. You don't think much about it. It's your tradition. It's what you are."[10] Her youth was defined by regimented attendance at 10 a.m. Sunday Mass, nightly prayers, family rosary, and Blessed Virgin statues in every room of the home.

Yet her parents, "although they were Catholics to the letter of the law, were extremely tolerant, discussed things, and did not worship the clergy."[11] The "ritual of the church" was both essential and not center; part of their cultural and familial identity, but not "a burden."[12] "As a result," McDermott reflects, her parents made Catholic faith "something I could think about and reject at times and go back to, and not something so controlling that I would either have to accept it fully or reject it fully. They conveyed a sense of what is essential to the church, and what is part of but not essential to it."[13]

Her youthful rebellion meant trips to Dunkin Donuts when she was supposed to be at Mass. Like others, she and her friends "thought we were the first people in the history of the universe ever to question" the Church.[14] When she started attending Catholic school, "nuns wore long habits and were mysterious. By the time I finished, they were in business suits and were taking us to Greenwich Village to art galleries and soup kitchens."[15] Inspired by Vatican II, the nuns who taught her were enthusiastic, "very sincere, and they wanted to engage us in discussions about everything. Our turning away, or scorn, or intolerance, had more to do with adolescence than theology."[16]

McDermott found herself, like other Catholics of her generation, "edging back to the formal church as my children were born."[17] She thought of the trajectory of her own life, and considered that "if I give them this," the Catholic faith, "at least they'll have something to rebel against. I say, give them faith; let them have the same journey my contemporaries had, even if it's toward a rejection of it."[18] For McDermott, being Catholic means being aware that the religion's tensions and distresses are as present as the faith's requisite joys. She calls herself a "reluctant, resigned, occasionally exasperated but nevertheless practicing Catholic with no thought, or hope, of being otherwise."[19]

Her resignation comes from her sense of perspective: "I see the church not as something that *can* evolve, but something that *must* evolve. The church has been so wrong so many times, and has corrected itself, sometimes more thoroughly than others. The church is human, you know."[20] McDermott speaks of ritual and the liturgical year as creating the structural fabric for existence. Catholics "pause and think about the death on the cross, the resurrection, the birth, the parables"—their lives are bound by story, drama, and abstraction.[21]

There is no Catholicism without story. "Literature," McDermott explains, "spoke of the undeniable fears and longings of being human: the fear that we are, ultimately, lost, ineffectual, trumped in all our pursuits and passions by death, though longing to discover otherwise."[22] McDermott realized that her "church, Catholicism, gave certain of my characters a language they could use in order to talk about, and to think about, this longing."[23]

At the same time, McDermott saw,

> that the language of the church, my church, was not only a means to an end in my fiction but an essential part of my own understanding of the world . . . I had come to see that the life of Christ, the Son of God whose death redeemed our lives, redeemed from absurdity our love for one another, made of our existence a perfect, artistic whole that satisfied, in a way that great art could only briefly satisfy, our hearts' persistent, insatiable need for meaning, for redemption.[24]

A powerful synthesis, certainly—and yet one that has begun to feel inevitable in American Catholic fiction. The spiritual and liturgical elements of Catholicism—sinners paired with saints, the sacred intermingling with the damned, abstraction captured in the whispers of ritual, the communal experience—make the faith almost fuel for artists. DeLillo, Pynchon, Morrison, McCarthy, and Erdrich drifted from the Church while retaining, and being charged by, its symbolism; McDermott, in contrast, is a practicing, public Catholic. She is pulled, but not torn, in her relationship with the Church.

"Catholicism, I began to see, was also mine, inextricably mine, the fabric of my life and my thoughts."[25] She knew there were other languages for faith, ones that might have been "more effective, less burdened by nonessentials, perhaps even superior to the language the Catholic church had provided me, but I would have to live another life entirely in order to know them and to feel them as deeply or as inevitably as I knew and felt my Catholic faith. Resignation and delight: I am a Catholic after all. My only obligation, my profound obligation, is to make the best of it."[26]

She has done so in her fiction. Her finest and most-lauded novel, the National Book Award–winning *Charming Billy* (1998), is both expansive and particular—a testament to McDermott's storytelling gifts. In novels, her cultural Catholicism is both atmospheric—arising from ritual, setting, and sensory detail— and a source of morality for her characters. It doesn't mean that her characters act traditionally Catholic in terms of their morality, but rather that the moral code is present in their lives. Catholicism, she has said, gives her characters "a vocabulary that they might not otherwise have."[27] Her characters wrangle with and articulate the complexities of their lives within a Catholic language. They "would not know how to say, 'There's got to be something more than this,' or 'I've found something more than this,' if they couldn't also say 'redemption' or 'ascension.'"[28] Faith gives "language to our common experience of uncertainty, of yearning."[29]

Charming Billy is a story of that yearning, that longing— of things both sacred and sensual. McDermott has a talent for writing about seemingly unassuming, average lives by finding the contours of their hope and grief. Maeve Lynch is the widow of Billy Lynch, a man who had "drunk himself to death," having "ripped apart, plowed through, as alcoholics tend to do, the great, deep, tightly woven fabric of affection that was some part of the emotional life, the life of love, of everyone in the room."[30]

That room is the reception after Billy's funeral. There is eating, drinking, and talking—much talk of "the Irish girl," Eva, whom

Billy loved before he met his wife Maeve. The novel is narrated by the daughter of Dennis Lynch, Billy's cousin and best friend, and she captures the hidden conversation that unfolds in Maeve's presence. "If Eva had been the beauty," the narrator says, "then Maeve was only a faint consolation, a futile attempt to mend an irreparably broken heart. A moment's grace, a flash of optimism, not enough for a lifetime."[31]

Young Maeve is described as "a plain girl, but determined."[32] The daughter of a policeman, Maeve "had gotten some sense early on of the precariousness of life, the risk taken by simply walking out the apartment door."[33] As a child she was "wedded" to her "widowed father," who needed her to spend extra hours at school with the nuns.[34] She'd sit for hours in the courtyard with "vine-covered walls, a single oak, a statue of St. Francis above a concrete birdbath, one of the Virgin in the crook of the tree," or even in the front room, "where the silence was palpable, luxurious, punctuated as it was by the soft steps of the sisters going through the hall or up the stairs or stopping in to bring her a glass of ginger ale and some digestive biscuits on a saucer."[35]

In contrast, Eva's Irishness is presented as exotic and mysterious. Danny Lynch, another cousin, said that he went to the Feast of the Assumption Mass with Billy once. "I glanced at Billy, just after Communion. It struck me that it wasn't any thought of Our Lord or the Blessed Mother that put the look on his face. It was the girl. The Irish girl. When he turned his eyes to heaven, that's who he saw."[36]

Billy and Eva's story began after Billy, like his cousin Dennis, returned home from the war. The cousins were both still virgins, and had "bruised girls' lips with kisses" but "the Paulist Fathers had gotten them at an early age and they had studied heaven and hell long before they knew that at the top of a stocking there was only bare flesh."[37] Out in the city at midnight, "as drunk as the girls on their knees," Billy and Dennis "saw through the bold music and the laughter and the smoky air their foreshortened lives, the nearness of eternity, and so always rode the subway home alone, reeling and laughing and helped by the hands of innumerable smiling strangers, to sleep it off under their mothers' own roof."[38]

After he got back from the war, Billy started going to daily Mass. Like other veterans, he had "a new sense that only the daily, formal petition for mercy would get them through the rest of their lives."[39] That routine included "the good sound of the familiar Latin, the same women every morning saying their beads, the red sanctuary lamp, and the candles beneath the statues of the Virgin and St. Joseph, steadfast and true."[40] When Billy meets Eva, he falls fast and hard. She returns to Ireland, but they plan to marry, so Billy sends her money. Tragically, she dies of pneumonia, and Dennis has to deliver the news to a heartbroken Billy.

Except it was all a lie. Dennis doesn't tell his daughter, the novel's narrator, the truth until the end of the funeral reception. Eva married a man in Ireland, and kept Billy's money. Death, for Dennis, seemed a better story than the truth of Eva's betrayal. Billy learns the truth himself years later during a trip to Ireland. There is no grand embrace; no rekindling of love. Sometimes life drifts away from us, McDermott suggests, and we are left only with regret and longing.

After the funeral reception, a priest comes to the Lynch's home. The narrator describes how "Maeve put both her hands out for the priest and the priest stepped toward her easily, confidently, like an expert, a pro. . . . We all felt it, felt the tremendous sense of relief that we finally had among us someone who knew what he was doing."[41] "It's a terrible thing, Father," Maeve says to him, "To come this far in life only to find that nothing you've felt has made any difference."[42]

The priest tells everyone to say a rosary with him, thinking "the repetitiveness of the prayers, the hushed drone of repeated, and by its numbing repetition, nearly wordless, supplication, was the only antidote, tonight, for Maeve's hopelessness." They collect chairs from the dining room and "a kind of circle formed, although this was not the sort of Catholic gathering where anyone would think to join hands."[43] The line brings to mind Billy himself, who didn't like AA meetings, calling it "a Protestant thing."[44] He "could tell who the Catholics were because they'd all been bowing their heads every ten seconds while the Protestants bantered on about Jesus, Jesus, Jesus."[45]

After the prayers end, the conversations settle into their own corners, and some women think about how "Maeve had known all along about the Irish girl, and still she had given Billy her heart."[46] *Charming Billy* unfolds like a long sigh: the recognition that life rarely happens as planned, and yet characters like Billy and Maeve find subtle comforts. It is a melancholic feel that also describes *Someone*, McDermott's 2013 novel. In the first scene, Marie is sitting on the stoop of her Brooklyn home, waiting for her father. She is shy, quiet, and 7 years old. She sees two "Sisters of Charity from the convent down the street" pass, "smiling from inside their bonnets."[47] She waits "for the first sighting of my father, coming up from the subway in his hat and coat, most beloved among all those ghosts."[48]

Her childhood apartment was "long and narrow," and the back "caught the morning light," although that light permeated the apartment: the windows, the carpet, the dining-room chairs and table.[49] "It was the first light my poor eyes ever knew," Marie says.[50] "Recalling it, I sometimes wonder if all the faith and all the fancy, all the fear, the speculation, all the wild imaginings that go into the study of heaven and hell, don't shortchange, after all, that other, earlier uncertainty: the darkness before the slow coming to awareness of the first light."[51] In that apartment, her brother, Gabe, recites poetry at dinner. Her "parents might have seen the priest in him then, the way he stood at the end of the table, offered up the lovely words."[52]

Outside, Marie still smells the vinegar that a woman who died had used to clean her windows. She describes it as an "Easter scent, I thought, although Easter had already passed. It was the scent of the solution we made to dye our eggs, but also the odor that pricked my nose in church when they read that part of the Passion where Jesus said, I thirst, and a sponge soaked with wine and vinegar was raised to his lips. And then the angel in the empty tomb saying, 'He's not here.'"[53]

At seventeen, she meets a boy, Walter Hartnett, who breaks her heart. Her brother, Gabe, had become a priest, but leaves after a short time. Walter has left Marie for another girl, and she's hurt. Marie asks Gabe: "Who's going to love me?" "Someone," he responds. "Someone will."[54] It is a touching scene, a vision of Gabe's eternal priesthood, of a gentle optimism in the light of unforgiving reality.

We learn in the next chapter that someone did love Marie. She had four children, and lived the life that she'd longed for—but structurally, McDermott offers readers the conclusion before the developing story. McDermott is interested in showing us the small graces along the way. Years earlier, in order to protect Marie, Gabe cuts out Walter's wedding announcement from the newspaper. At first, she felt patronized, but appreciated the "generosity and futility" of her brother's actions.[55]

Marie gets a job working as a "consoling angel" for a local undertaker. She gains composure and confidence, and has no problem finding men to meet and date. "By the time I reached my twenties," Marie recalls, "my heartbreak was mended, I suppose—much as the notion of what might have been still lingered: the bright wedding in the pretty church, not to mention that house in the country—but I was no fool."[56] Gabe thinks his sister is trying "to make up for what happened with Walter," to "prove something about yourself," but she rejects his judgement.[57]

Later, on her wedding night, Marie was "naïve enough, drunk enough, to be surprised to find that a body could become a new thing altogether, shed of its clothes."[58] She thought of how movies depicted the wedding night as including "room service, a bell-hop pushing a cloth-draped table into the room, ostrich feathers on my sleeves, but it was Sunday morning and we had to fast, since we were meeting my mother and Gabe for ten o'clock Mass."[59]

Her father died while Gabe was still a priest; he'd given their father the last sacrament. Her mother says "I think it was the end of that poor boy's sweet faith, to see your father suffer the way he did. To see his body suffer. Here he was, newly minted, full up with all the words they'd given him out there, at the seminary, all the prayers, and here was the sight of his father's body reduced to a whimpering, suffering thing."[60]

It is a pungent, piercing scene that stays with Marie, and acutely resurfaces during her first childbirth, when she almost dies. "It was not that my life was less valuable to me now that I had glimpsed what it would be like to lose it," she says, but that love "was required of me now—to be given, not merely to be sought and returned. My presence on earth was never more urgently needed. And yet even the certainty of that fact seemed reason to throw away caution, not to heed it"—to have another child and risk death again.[61]

Later in the novel, Gabe has a nervous breakdown, and comes to stay with Marie, in scenes that hearken back to that dimly lit apartment of their youth. Marie's language is graceful and religious: "My brother was a mystery to me, but a mystery I had always associated with the sacred darkness of the bedroom we shared in Brooklyn, or the hushed grooves of the seminary, or the spice of the incense in the cavernous church, even with his lifelong, silent communion with the words he found in his books."[62] Her brother laid emotionally bare before her, Marie's "heart fell to think that the holy mystery of who my brother was might be made flesh, ordinary flesh, by the notion that he was simply a certain kind of man."[63]

In *Someone*, Marie is not overly pious, but her life has been shaped by her family's faith. Her language, her sense of being and hope, even her fits of melancholy, are patently Irish Catholic. McDermott's most recent novel, *The Ninth Hour* (2017), continues this trend, but does so with perhaps a more haunting tone. Cast largely with nuns and set in the early twentieth century, the novel shares Ron Hansen's ability within *Mariette in Ecstasy* to recreate a Catholic atmosphere in which faith suffused all things. Yet their styles and outcomes are very different. Hansen's paragraphs are peripatetic, their fragmentation a nod to the intertwining of doubt and belief. McDermott's prose is smooth and direct, which makes the accumulating turns of the novel all the more shocking. *The Ninth Hour* feels painfully real, the lives of its characters authentically messy. Salvation is just out of their reach.

The novel begins in early February: "Was there a moment of the year better suited for despair?"[64] Jim, a thirty-two-year-old Irish immigrant, is alone in his Brooklyn apartment. He'd convinced his pregnant wife, Annie, "to go out to do her shopping before darkness fell."[65] McDermott methodically traces his movements around the railroad flat, which includes reaching behind the stove and removing the gas hose from the tap. The scene is somehow surreal and precise: Jim walks with the hose, reminiscing about Annie and about how he'd recently lost his job. He sits on his bed, takes off his shoes, prays, and then puts the tube to his mouth. He stands again, looks out the window, and "watche[s] two nuns in black cloaks and white wimples, their heads bent together, skim over the gray sidewalk."[66]

Jim's suicide starts *The Ninth Hour* on a dark note, but there's never a macabre moment in McDermott's novel. That's a nod to the novelist's worldview, but also her method. In the next scene, we are introduced to Sister St. Saviour, a Little Nursing Sister of the Sick Poor. She is sixty-four, and has seen it all—addiction, injury, and death. As she enters Annie's apartment and moves past the police, she thinks not of judgment but of empathy: "We're all feeling it, she'd thought, in this vale of tears: the weight of the low sky and the listless rain and the damp depths of this endless winter."[67]

But this is her vocation, and her advice to Annie is blunt: "What we must do is to put one foot in front of the other."[68] For Annie, that means dinner and a place to stay—and, perhaps, a proper Christian burial for her husband, despite his final act. Sister St. Saviour wanted this to "give comfort to his poor wife," but also "because the power of the Church wanted him kept out and she, who had spent her life in the Church's service, wanted him in."[69]

Her optimism is tempered by the realism of other nuns, such as Sister Lucy, who think "all was thin ice."[70] Yet Lucy and the other women have their vocations, and they take in Annie, who is paid $18 a week and fed. Her infant daughter, Sally, sleeps in a wicker basket "fitted with towels and a pillowslip" while Annie does chores, including "help[ing] Sister Illuminata with the ironing."[71] Illuminata "was shrill in her demands, unbending in her routines."[72] McDermott places the women together "in the basement of the convent, amid the dampness and the rising steam, the baby asleep in her crib, the sheets or long johns hung out on the line," and offers a window into the world of these religious women.[73]

They were not born into this life, but they did not speak of the world before the convent: "The white horse-blinder bonnets they wore did more than limit their peripheral vision. They reminded the Sisters to look only at the work at hand."[74] The focus is on their labors, but emotions seep through. Sister Jeanne, "small and soft-spoken and easily given to laughter or tears," often watches young Sally in the afternoon.[75] Jeanne makes a "fairy story of sorts out of each of the Mysteries" of the Rosary while the girl falls asleep.[76] In those idle moments, Jeanne thinks of Jim, and how the "madness with which suffering was dispersed in the world defied logic."[77]

Jim's suicide reverberates throughout the novel, collapsing the expanding years of *The Ninth Hour*, like *That Night*, back into the importance of a single moment. The nuns often speak of the fairness of God, how their habitual devotion is buoyed by the hope that the divine tips the scales of human folly toward justice. A wish does not theology make—and a wish certainly does not bend the ecclesial authorities. Jim was refused a funeral Mass. In the thoughts of many of the nuns, and in the judgment of the Church, he had thrown his life away. Annie is left unmoored, her prayers to God left unanswered.

God's fairness might be complicated, but McDermott is a kind novelist—at least when it comes to giving her characters hope. Annie meets Mr. Costello, a milkman who offers her emotional escape. They are both suffering, but share "no mournful tales, then, of her widowhood, of his frail wife."[78] They spend a year talking with the comfortable distance of pleasant acquaintances, until one day she hands him the key to her apartment, and they both have a decision to make.

At the same time, Sally is growing up, and though she and Annie are growing closer—"More and more like sisters than mother and child," one woman notes—Sally is drawn to the religious life.[79] She spends recess in church, not playing with the other children. She tries on the habits of the Little Sisters. Illuminata quips to Annie: "Promised to Christ. . . . What man accepts a promise from a girl so young?"[80]

Annie is nervous. She doesn't want to be left alone again. Sally sees the religious life as sweet rebellion, and is coaxed on a bit by the sisters. In the modern world, after all, what could be more countercultural than devoting one's life to God? In the convent's basement, Illuminata sings the right tune: "Down here, we do our best to transform what is ugly, soiled, stained, don't we? We send it back into the world like a resurrected soul. We're like the priest in his confessional, aren't we?"[81] The old nun catches herself, but it might be too late. There's a fine line between the ideal and the real when one is intoxicated with the religious sense.

The Ninth Hour is a novel of questions, but it builds from a concrete statement: we are bound to our wounds from the past. McDermott spends the first half of the novel sufficiently convincing us that the twists and turns and heartbreaks of the second half are not simply plausible, but inevitable. The result is a fine novel and, perhaps surprisingly, a rather dark one. A life of devotion is no easy choice; one's vocation and will are continuously tested. As Jeanne tells Sally, "truth reveals itself."[82] McDermott's fiction consistently reminds us that truth is often uncomfortable.

This sense that the truth is uncomfortable permeates the fiction of another contemporary Catholic writer, Phil Klay. *Redeployment*, Klay's accomplished debut collection of stories, won the National Book Award in 2014. Born in Westchester, New York in 1983, Klay attended Regis High School, a Jesuit high school in New York City. Consistent with the Jesuit educational ethic, instruction at Regis was tied to a unified intellectual, moral, and spiritual identity, Klay says. He remembers reading "A Circle in the Fire" by Flannery O'Connor there, and the teacher told students to think of the story not as a riddle to be deciphered, but "as an experience that you're entering into."[83] Great advice: O'Connor's experiential fiction, of course, pairs well with the Ignatian dictum to find God in all things.

After Regis, Klay studied creative writing and literature at Dartmouth College, graduating in 2005. He was soon commissioned as a second lieutenant in the United States Marine Corps, and in 2007 was deployed to Iraq during the troop surge. He served as a public affairs officer out of Camp Taqaddum in Anbar Province until February 2008. Those experiences—infused with a Jesuit sensibility—became the stories of *Redeployment*. Klay's book of stories is visceral and violent, but presented with a complex religious sense that sets his book apart among contemporary fiction of war.

Klay has often talked about how veterans are seen as polarities: dangerous super-soldiers, or emotionally broken husks. They are unable to be human again. It is hard being a soldier, Klay argues, but it is also hard being a civilian. His fiction engages the murky morality within both worlds, and rejects the idea "that war is beyond words. I think that we like to imagine that it is. There's a kind of mysticism around war, but actually what it does is it builds a neat little box around the veteran. It shuts them up."[84] As a short-story collection, *Redeployment* offered Klay a multiplicity of voices within a shared experience. The varied stories in the collection also capture the range of religious experience, from skepticism to confusion to longing.

"Short fiction was essential for what I wanted to do with my book," Klay told me in an interview for *Image*. "I was originally working on a novel at the same time, but in an odd way I found the novel form too limiting. I didn't want a coherent narrative running through the collection. I wanted the twelve different voices to bounce off of each other and inform each other without being shoehorned into some sort of narrative arc. The disjoint felt right for the reading experience I wanted to create."[85]

In "After Action Report," a soldier narrates how a kid was shot during a firefight in Iraq. The kid had "grabbed his dad's AK when he saw us standing there and thought he'd be a hero and take a potshot at the Americans."[86] It was another soldier, Timhead, who killed the kid, but the narrator begins to take on the story as his own—speaking to how the guilt of war is infectious. The soldier speaks with the chaplain, explaining "every time I hear an explosion, I'm like, That could be one of my friends. And when I'm on a convoy, every time I see a pile of trash or rocks or dirt, I'm like, That could be me."[87] The chaplain, in turn, suggests prayer, but the narrator is skeptical. He imagines prayer to be superstitious; a charm against evil. "That's not what prayer's for," the chaplain explains: "It will not protect you . . . It's about your relationship with God."[88] He continues, "It will help your soul. It's for while you're alive. . . . It's for while you're dead, too, I guess."[89]

"Prayer in the Furnace," one of the longest stories in the collection, is narrated by a priest. A soldier named Rodriguez approaches the priest at the start of the story, "blood smeared across his face in horizontal and diagonal streaks. His hands and sleeves were stained, and he wouldn't look at me directly, his eyes wild and empty."[90] He "only wanted a cigarette," and it wasn't until the chaplain stood that the soldier "saw the cross on my collar."[91]

Soon after, during a funeral for the battalion's twelfth soldier killed in action, the priest reads from 2 Timothy: "I have fought the good fight. I have finished the race. I have kept the faith."[92] His elegiac words are followed by the Charlie Company commander, who talks of only revenge. At the end of the service, the soldiers go to the battle cross and kneel together, "arms over one another's shoulders, leaning into one another until it was one silent, weeping block. Geared up, Marines are terrifying warriors. In grief, they look like children."[93]

Afterward, the chaplain thinks about how he never goes on combat missions. Despite feeling overworked and emotionally drained, he is safe, only hearing violence "in the distance."[94] The priest feels much like Saint Augustine, "sermonizing from safety about the sack of his beloved Rome," saying: "Horrible it was told to us; the slaughter, burning, pillaging, the torture of men. It is true, many things we have heard, all filled with bellowing, weeping, and hardly were we comforted."[95] The chaplain feels inauthentic, in some ways—not quite a part of the war.

Rodriguez, from earlier in the story, comes to visit him in the chapel. The soldier says he respects priests, but not pedophiles and gay priests—his coarseness a "testing" of the chaplain.[96] He reveals what really happened when the recent soldier died. A corporal, high on Ambien, had climbed to a roof, and wearing only "underwear and Kevlar," he "starts doing jumping jacks, screaming every Arabic curse word he knows."[97] The soldiers were baiting insurgents: "We went out and found the enemy, instead of waiting for him to IED us. And our stats went up."[98]

In the midst of his explanation, Rodriguez makes a statement rather than a question: "If you killed somebody, that means you're going to hell."[99] The statement confuses the priest, who thinks Rodriguez is talking about the soldier's killing, but he means otherwise. The priest stumbles, saying "What are you telling me, Lance Corporal?"—his words arriving "in an officer voice, not in a pastoral voice."[100] The mangled conversation ends abruptly, and the priest is haunted by the soldier's words.

Distraught, the priest feels like he should do something, but he doesn't know who to talk to, skeptical of leadership who "looked at chaplains as the pray-at-ceremonies guys, not as trusted advisers."[101] The only possibility is his operations officer, a Catholic convert named Major Eklund. The major doesn't take kindly to the chaplain's insinuation that an investigation of Charlie Company is needed, and chides the chaplain for his naïve approach to battle. "Look, Father," he explains, "In a war like this, there's no easy answer. Neighborhood gets roughed up, sometimes. Sometimes, by accident, there's civilian casualties. It's not our fault."[102] He has little time for what he perceives to be the sheltered nuances of the chaplain's battlefield theology: "Look, Chaps, you have no idea what these guys are dealing with."[103]

After two more casualties, the priest prayed for "God to protect the battalion from further harm" but "knew He would not. I asked him to bring abuses to light. I knew He would not. I asked Him, finally, for grace."[104]

Mired in bureaucracy, his admonitions ignored, the priest thinks of a quote from St. Thomas Aquinas: "The sensitive appetite, though it obeys the reason, yet in a given case can resist by desiring what the reason forbids."[105] Bad conduct in war "is understandable, human, and so not a problem. If men inevitably act this way under stress, is it even a sin?"[106] His questions are rhetorical; even God, it seems, has no answers.

In his journal, the priest writes "I have this sense that this place is holier than back home. Gluttonous, fat, oversexed, overconsuming, materialist home, where we're too lazy to see our own faults. At least here, Rodriguez has the decency to worry about hell."[107]

What interests the priest about Rodriguez is that the soldier is at least willing to entertain the possibility that evil exists. Their conversations are dances of despair and theology—when Rodriguez, angry, says that the chaplain can't really help because he's a priest who has to "keep your hands clean," the chaplain says "No one's hands are clean except Christ's."[108] When Rodriguez says he doesn't think about God anymore, only the dead soldier, the chaplain says grace allows him to do that, to hold on to the memory. After the conversation, he thinks about the folly of the comforts he's offering. For those struggling, they must think if "God is real, there must be some consolation on earth as well. Some grace. Some evidence of mercy."[109]

He writes to Father Connelly, a Jesuit who was his high school Latin teacher, about how to minister to men who continue to suffer. The Jesuit tells the chaplain to temper his perception of justice, and be not "inclined to lose your pity for human weakness."[110] The priest needs "to find a crack through which some sort of communication can be made, one soul to another."[111]

More deaths follow, both during their service in Iraq, and when they return back home. A few soldiers kill themselves, including Rodriguez's old squad leader. After that, Rodriguez goes to see the priest, now at Camp Lejeune. He seems wracked with guilt, angry, and confused. The priest asks if the soldier wants to confess—"I think I wanted him to confess as much for my good as for his. It didn't really matter to me if he didn't think he believed anymore. Belief can come through process."[112]

"In this world," the priest says, holding the cross on his collar, "He only promises we don't suffer alone."[113] Rodriguez, turns, spits on the grass, and says "great."[114] The story ends abruptly. We are given no conclusions, no respite.

"Catholic literature takes the idea of sin seriously," Klay says. "It pays serious attention to suffering, to human fallibility, and the importance of ritual and community in human life,"[115] but Catholic fiction—any fiction—"is not there to instruct the reader with moral lessons."[116] *Redeployment* is absent of moral lessons, but not amoral. When I asked Klay how he sees faith entering the conversation about how we perceive and treat veterans, or how we talk about war, he said "there's the feeling of being trapped inside one's experience, which I address as both an interpersonal and political problem [in his writing]. But it's also a religious problem, insofar as being part of most religious practices means being part of a community."[117]

Klay quotes Pope Paul VI's document from Vatican II, *Lumen Gentium*, which says, "By communicating His Spirit, Christ made His brothers, called together from all nations, mystically the components of His own Body. In that Body the life of Christ is poured into the believers who, through the sacraments, are united in a hidden and real way to Christ who suffered and was glorified."[118] Faith, then, establishes "a sense of both solidarity with veterans and implication alongside them."[119] Much in the same way his teacher told students to experience O'Connor's fiction from within, Klay's fiction places readers in war by putting us there: body, mind, and soul.

Although their settings and subjects differ, McDermott, Klay, and Hansen share a uniquely Catholic approach to fiction.

Catholicism is not merely ornamental or metaphorical. McDermott says it well: "What makes me a Catholic writer, I think, is not that these characters belong to a certain church, or neighborhood or time or place. What makes me a Catholic writer is that the faith I profess contends that out of love—love—for such troubled, flawed, struggling human beings, the Creator, the First Cause, became flesh so that we, every one of us, would not perish. I am a Catholic writer because this very notion—whether it be made up or divinely revealed, fanciful thinking or breathtaking truth—so astonishes me that I can't help but bring it to every story I tell."[120]

Astonish is an apt word. For McDermott, Klay, and Hansen, their astonishment serves an aesthetic purpose. The sincerity of their literary faiths make their works devotional, but not in a pedantic way; they are bearing literary witness to the power of story. For a practicing Catholic fiction writer, Christ is metaphor, body, symbol, blood, breath; Christ is all. It is a paradox, but one that resides in the ambiguity that is required of faith.

The writers included in *Longing for an Absent God* show that contemporary Catholic literature is sustained by the interplay between works by practicing Catholics, and those by cultural Catholics. While a similar statement might be true for other denominations and religions, the curious suffusion of Catholicism into one's culture and worldview—that one is "Catholic for life," and that a Catholic worldview transcends the lived practice of Catholic belief—has resulted in a rich and diverse literature that continues to make a significant contribution to American letters. Practicing or lapsed, Catholic writers long for God, and their longing creates a beautiful and melancholy story.

NOTES

Preface

1. H.L. Mencken, On Politics: A Carnival of Buncombe, ed. Malcolm Moos (Baltimore: Johns Hopkins University Press, 2006), 205.

2. Robert A. Slayton, Empire Statesman: The Rise and Redemption of Al Smith (New York: Simon & Schuster, 2001), 43.

3. Slayton, Empire Statesman, 45.

4. Slayton, Empire Statesman, 33.

5. Slayton, Empire Statesman, 147.

6. Slayton, Empire Statesman, xiv.

7. Fulton J. Sheen, Treasure in Clay: The Autobiography of Fulton J. Sheen. (New York: Random House, 2009), 66.

8. Sheen, Treasure in Clay, 65.

9. Alton J. Pelowski, "Remembering Mr. Blue," Columbia Online, June 1, 2014 https://tinyurl.com/y48p68fn.

10. Pelowski, "Rembering Mr. Blue."

11. Bernard Bergonzi, David Lodge (Devon: Northcote House Publishers, 1995), 43.

12. Myles Connolly, Mr. Blue (Chicago: Loyola Press, 2004), 5.

13. Connolly, Mr. Blue, 44.

14. Connolly, Mr. Blue, 28.

15. Connolly, Mr. Blue, 13.

16. Connolly, Mr. Blue, 10.

17. Connolly, Mr. Blue, 14.

18. Connolly, Mr. Blue, 15.

19. Connolly, Mr. Blue, 15.

20. Connolly, Mr. Blue, 91.

21. Connolly, Mr. Blue, 91.

22. Connolly, Mr. Blue, 91.

23. Connolly, Mr. Blue, 91.

24. Connolly, Mr. Blue, 93.

Introduction

1. Flannery O'Connor, A Prayer Journal (New York: Farrar, Straus and Giroux: 2013), 36.

2. Flannery O'Connor, Mystery and Manners: Occasional Prose (New York: Farrar, Straus and Giroux, 1969), 20.

3. O'Connor, Mystery and Manners, 31.

4. O'Connor, Mystery and Manners ,153.

5. O'Connor, Mystery and Manners, 153.

6. O'Connor, Mystery and Manners, 156.

7. O'Connor, Mystery and Manners, 34.

8. O'Connor, Mystery and Manners, 145.

9. O'Connor, Mystery and Manners, 145.

10. O'Connor, Mystery and Manners, 162.

11. Paul Elie, "What Flannery Knew," Commonweal, November 21, 2008, 12.

12. Dana Gioia, The Catholic Writer Today and Other Essays (Belmont, NC: Wiseblood, 2019), 17.

13. Elie, "What Flannery Knew," 27.

14. Elie, "What Flannery Knew," 21.

15. Elie, "What Flannery Knew," 21.

16. Don DeLillo, White Noise (New York: Viking, 1998), 316.

17. DeLillo, White Noise, 317.

18. DeLillo, White Noise, 318.

19. DeLillo, White Noise, 318.

20. DeLillo, White Noise, 319.

21. DeLillo, White Noise, 320.

22. DeLillo, White Noise, 320.

23. Don DeLillo, Mao II (New York: Scribner, 1991), 16.

24. Adam Begley, "Don DeLillo: The Art of Fiction," The Paris Review (Fall 1993), https://tinyurl.com/y2yxuwae.

25. Robert Harris, "A Talk with Don DeLillo," The New York Times (October 10, 1982), BR26.

26. Don DeLillo, Conversations with Don DeLillo. Edited by Thomas DePietro (Jackson: University Press of Mississippi, 2005), 10.

27. DeLillo, Conversations with Don DeLillo.

28. Don DeLillo, Underworld (New York: Scribner, 1997), 821.

29. DeLillo, Underworld, 821.

30. DeLillo, Underworld, 821.

31. DeLillo, Underworld, 824.

32   Don DeLillo, End Zone (New York: Penguin, 1972), 10.

33   DeLillo, End Zone, 19.

34   DeLillo End Zone, 19.

35   DeLillo, End Zone, 30.

36   DeLillo, End Zone, 31.

37   DeLillo, End Zone, 56.

38   DeLillo, End Zone, 233.

39   DeLillo, End Zone, 233.

40   DeLillo, End Zone, 233.

41   DeLillo, End Zone, 195.

42   DeLillo, End Zone, 64.

43   DeLillo, End Zone, 241.

44   DeLillo, End Zone, 239.

45   DeLillo, End Zone, 240.

46   DeLillo, End Zone, 242.

47   Pierre Teilhard de Chardin, The Phenomenon of Man (New York: Harper & Row, 1975), 259.

48   Thomas DePietro, "Everyday Mysteries," America, April 30, 2012, https://tinyurl.com/yyyx6lfd.

49   Alexandra Alter, "What Don DeLillo's Books Tell Him," The Wall Street Journal, January 30, 2010, https://tinyurl.com/y6ev3lrj.

50   DeLillo, End Zone, 56.

51   DeLillo, End Zone, 196.

52   Ron Hansen, A Stay Against Confusion: Essays on Faith and Fiction (New York: HarperPerennial, 2001), 18.

53   Hansen, A Stay Against Confusion, 19.

54   Hansen, A Stay Against Confusion, 259.

55   Hansen, A Stay Against Confusion, 4.

56   Ron Hansen, Mariette in Ecstasy (New York: HarperPerennial, 1991), 23.

57   Hansen, Mariette in Ecstasy, 11.

58   Hansen, Mariette in Ecstasy, 35.

59   Hansen, Mariette in Ecstasy, 35.

60   Tom De Haven, "Mariette in Ecstasy," Entertainment Weekly, November 1, 1991, https://tinyurl.com/y4ycoc8s.

61   Michiko Kakutani, "In a Convent, Rapture and Questions of Reality," The New York Times, November 5, 1991, C17.

62   Kakutani, "In A Convent, Rapture and Questions of Reality."

63   Hansen, Mariette, 31.

64   Hansen, Mariette, 9

65   Hansen, Mariette, 19.

66   Hansen, Mariette, 36.

67   Hansen, Mariette, 16.

68   Hansen, Mariette, 62.

69   Hansen, Mariette, 92.

70   Hansen, Mariette, 92.

71   Hansen, Mariette, 57.

72   Hansen, Mariette, 121.

73   Hansen, Mariette, 107.

74   Hansen, Mariette, 112.

75   Hansen, Mariette, 150.

76   Hansen, Mariette, 150.

77   Hansen, Mariette, 125.

78   Hansen, Mariette, 125.

79   Hansen, Mariette, 173.

80   Hansen, Mariette, 179.

81   Hansen, Mariette, 179.

Chapter 1

1   Graham Greene, The Comedians (New York: Penguin, 1966), 61.

2   Graham Greene, The Graham Greene Film Reader, ed. David Parkinson (Montclair: Applause Books, 1994), 385.

3   Greene, Graham Greene Film Reader, xiv.

4   Greene, Graham Greene Film Reader, xiv.

5   Graham Greene, "On Becoming a Catholic," Commonweal 94 (1971): https://tinyurl.com/yyucnh24.

6   Greene, "Becoming a Catholic."

7   Greene, "Becoming a Catholic."

8   Greene, "Becoming a Catholic."

9   Greene, "Becoming a Catholic."

10   Greene, "Becoming a Catholic."

11   Greene, "Becoming a Catholic."

12   Greene, "Becoming a Catholic."

13   Greene, "Becoming a Catholic."

14   Greene, "Becoming a Catholic."

15   Greene, "Becoming a Catholic."

16   Greene, "Becoming a Catholic."

17   Graham Greene, Conversations with Graham Greene, ed. Henry J. Donaghy (Jackson: University Press of Mississippi, 1992), 26.

18 Graham Greene, Travels with My Aunt (New York: Viking, 1970), 135.

19 Greene, Travels, 117.

20 Marie-Françoise Allain, "The Uneasy Catholicism of Graham Greene," The New York Times, April, 3, 1983, 21.

21 Greene, Conversations, 86.

22 Allain, "Uneasy Catholicism," 11.

23 Allain, "Uneasy Catholicism," 11.

24 Greene, Conversations, 48.

25 Norman Sherry, The Life of Graham Greene Volume Two: 1939–1955 (New York: Random House, 2016), 43.

26 Sherry, The Life, 43.

27 Graham Greene, The Power and the Glory (New York: Penguin, 2003), 65.

28 Greene, The Power, 157.

29 Greene, The Power, 130.

30 Greene, The Power, 130.

31 Greene, The Power, 130.

32 Greene, The Power, 97.

33 Greene, The Power, 97.

34 Greene, Conversations, 78.

35 Greene, Conversations, 78.

36 Greene, Conversations, 141.

37 Flannery O'Connor, The Habit of Being, ed. Sally Fitzgerald (New York: Farrar, Straus & Giroux, 1979), 231.

38 Flannery O'Connor, Mystery and Manners, ed. Sally Fitzgerald and Robert Fitzgerald (New York: Farrar, Straus & Giroux, 1969), 232.

39 O'Connor, The Habit of Being, 139.

40 O'Connor, The Habit of Being, 98.

41 O'Connor, The Habit of Being, 119.

42 O'Connor, The Habit of Being, 201.

43 O'Connor, The Habit of Being, 120–21.

44 O'Connor, The Habit of Being, 400.

45 O'Connor, Mystery and Manners, 34.

46 O'Connor, Mystery and Manners, 90.

47 O'Connor, The Habit of Being 517.

48 Brad Gooch, Flannery: A Life of Flannery O'Connor (New York: Little, Brown, 2009), 363.

49 David R. Mayer, "Outer Marks, Inner Grace: Flannery O'Connor's Tattooed Christ," Asian Folklore Studies 42, no. 1 (1983): 119.

50 Mayer, "Outer Marks," 120.

51 Flannery O'Connor, The Correspondence of Flannery O'Connor and the Brainard Cheneys, ed. C. Ralph Stephens (Jackson: University Press of Mississippi, 1986), 187.

52 Gooch, Flannery, 364.

53 Gooch, Flannery, 366.

54 Flannery O'Connor, The Complete Stories (New York: Farrar, Straus & Giroux, 1982), 512, 513.

55 O'Connor, Complete Stories, 512, 513.

56 O'Connor, Complete Stories, 513.

57 O'Connor, Complete Stories, 514.

58 O'Connor, Complete Stories, 514.

59 O'Connor, Complete Stories, 518.

60 O'Connor, Complete Stories, 517.

61 O'Connor, Complete Stories, 519.

62 O'Connor, Complete Stories, 522.

63 O'Connor, Complete Stories, 522.

64 O'Connor, Complete Stories, 522.

65 O'Connor, Complete Stories, 523.

66 O'Connor, Complete Stories, 524.

67 O'Connor, Complete Stories, 529.

68 O'Connor, Complete Stories, 529.

69 O'Connor, Complete Stories, 529.

70 O'Connor, Complete Stories, 529.

71 Galatians 6:11. All biblical quotes are from the NAB, 1991.

72 Galatians 6:17.

Chapter 2

1 Rust Hills, "The Structure of the American Literary Establishment: Who Makes or Breaks a Writer's Reputation? A Chart of Power," Esquire, July 1963, 41.

2 O'Connor, The Habit of Being, 526.

3 O'Connor, Mystery and Manners, 159.

4 Paul Elie, The Life You Save May Be Your Own: An American Pilgrimage (New York: Farrar, Straus & Giroux, 204), 337.

5 O'Connor, Mystery and Manners, 58–59.

6 Walker Percy, Conversations with Walker Percy, ed. Lewis A. Lawson and Victor A. Kramer (Jackson: University Press of Mississippi, 1985), 4.

7 Percy, Conversations, 96–97.

8 Percy, Conversations, 186.

9   Walker Percy, More Conversations with Walker Percy, ed. Lewis A. Lawson and Victor A. Kramer (Jackson: University Press of Mississippi, 1993) 22.

10 Percy, More Conversations, 218.

11 Walker Percy, Signposts in a Strange Land (New York: Farrar, Straus & Giroux ,1991), 343.

12 Percy, More Conversations, 126.

13 Percy, More Conversations, 126.

14 Percy, Conversations, 88.

15 Percy, Conversations, 274.

16 Percy, Conversations, 9.

17 Percy, More Conversations, 233.

18 Percy, Conversations, 73.

19 Percy, Conversations, 41.

20 Percy, Conversations, 41.

21 Percy, More Conversations, 5–6.

22 Percy, More Conversations, 27.

23 Percy, More Conversations, 122.

24 Percy, More Conversations, 205.

25 Percy, Conversations, 28–29.

26 Percy, Signposts, 36.

27 Percy, Signposts, 36.

28 Walker Percy, The Moviegoer (New York: Vintage, 1998), 5.

29 Percy, The Moviegoer, 4.

30 Percy, The Moviegoer, 5.

31 Percy, The Moviegoer, 7.

32 Percy, The Moviegoer, 75.

33 Percy, The Moviegoer, 7.

34 Percy, The Moviegoer, 7.

35 Percy, The Moviegoer, 73.

36 Percy, The Moviegoer, 73.

37 Percy, The Moviegoer, 73.

38 Percy, The Moviegoer, 73, 74.

39 Percy, The Moviegoer, 143.

40 Percy, The Moviegoer, 79.

41 Percy, The Moviegoer, 79.

42 Percy, Conversations, 13.

43 Percy, The Moviegoer 48.

44 Percy, The Moviegoer, 48.

45 Percy, The Moviegoer, 52.

46 Percy, The Moviegoer, 142.

47 Percy, The Moviegoer, 142.

48 Percy, The Moviegoer, 159.

49 Percy, The Moviegoer, 159.

50 Percy, More Conversations, 126.

51 Percy, The Moviegoer, 228.

52 Percy, The Moviegoer, 233.

53 Percy, The Moviegoer, 235.

54 Percy, The Moviegoer, 235.

55 Percy, The Moviegoer, 235.

56 Percy, The Moviegoer, 88.

57 Percy, Signposts, 368.

58 Andre Dubus, "Paths to Redemption," Harper's, April 1977, 88.

59 Dubus, "Paths to Redemption," 86.

60 Dubus, "Paths to Redemption," 86.

61 Dubus, "Paths to Redemption," 86.

62 Bill Buford, "Editorial," Granta 8 (Autumn 1983), 4.

63 Buford, "Editorial," 4.

64 Buford, "Editorial," 4.

65 John T. McGreevy, Catholicism and American Freedom (New York: W.W. Norton, 2003), 270.

66 Jon Holmes, "With Andre Dubus," Boston Review 9, no. 4 (July–August 1984): 8.

67 Holmes, "With Andre Dubus," 8.68 Andre Dubus, Conversations with Andre Dubus, ed. Olivia Carr Edenfield (Jackson: University Press of Mississippi, 2013), 61.

69 Andre Dubus, Meditations from a Movable Chair (New York: Vintage, 1999), 19.

70 Dubus, Meditations, 24.

71 Dubus, Meditations, 30.

72 Dubus, Meditations, 32.

73 Dubus, Meditations, 32.

74 Andre Dubus, Selected Stories (New York: Vintage, 1996), 83.

75 Dubus, Selected Stories, 87.

76 Andre Dubus, Broken Vessels (Boston: David R. Godine, 1991), xv.

77 Dubus, Selected Stories, 393.

78 Dubus, Broken Vessels, 77.

79 Dubus, Broken Vessels, 77.

80 Dubus, Broken Vessels, 77.

81 Michael Reynolds, Hemingway: The Homecoming (New York: W.W. Norton, 1999), 156.

82 Dubus, Conversations, 19.

83 Dubus, Conversations, 371.

84 Dubus, Conversations, 373.

85 Andre Dubus, The Times Are Never So Bad (Boston: David R. Godine, 1983), 61.

86 Dubus, Selected Stories, 456.

87 Dubus, Selected Stories, 456.

88 Dubus, Selected Stories, 457.

89 Dubus, Selected Stories, 474.

90 Dubus, Selected Stories, 475.

91 Dubus, Selected Stories, 475.

92 Dubus, Selected Stories, 476.

93 Dubus, Conversations, 27.

94 Dubus, Broken Vessels, 127.

95 Dubus, Conversations, 196.

96 Walker Percy, The Message in the Bottle (New York: Farrar, Straus & Giroux, 1989), 111.

97 Dubus, Conversations, 246.

98 Dubus, Selected Stories, 160.

Chapter 3

1 Ian Froeb, "Don DeLillo Accepts St. Louis University Literary Award," Riverfront Times, October 22, 2010, https://tinyurl.com/yyn4p8hb.

2 M. Chénétier and F. Happe, "An Interview with Don DeLillo," Revue française d'études américaines, January 2001, 107.

3 Chénétier and Happe, "Interview," 109.

4 Don DeLillo, Conversations with Don DeLillo, ed. Thomas DePietro (Jackson: University Press of Mississippi, 2005), 81.

5 DeLillo, Conversations, 4.

6 James Joyce, A Portrait of the Artist as a Young Man, (New York: B. W. Huebsch, 1916), 291.

7 James Joyce, The Letters of James Joyce, Volume 2, ed. Richard Ellmann (New York: Viking, 1966), 48.

8 Quoted in Richard Ellmann, James Joyce (Oxford: Oxford University Press, 1965), 27.

9 DeLillo, Conversations, 10.

10 DeLillo, Conversations, 16.

11 DeLillo, Conversations, 128.

12 DeLillo, Conversations, 138.

13 DeLillo, Conversations, 138.

14 DeLillo, Conversations, 138.

15 Thomas DePietro, "Everyday Mysteries," America, April 30, 2012, https://tinyurl.com/yyyx6lfd.

16 Pope John Paul XXIII, "Announcement of an Ecumenical Council," https://tinyurl.com/y4nq5cqp.

17 Don DeLillo, Americana (New York: Penguin, 1971), 3.

18 DeLillo, Americana, 3.

19 DeLillo, Americana, 29.

20 DeLillo, Americana, 85.

21 M. Chénétier and F. Happe, "Interview," 107.

22 DeLillo, Americana 130.

23 DeLillo, Americana, 131.

24 DeLillo, Americana, 138.

25 DeLillo, Americana, 138.

26 DeLillo, Americana, 179.

27 DeLillo, Americana, 179.

28 DeLillo, Americana, 155.

29 DeLillo, Americana, 156.

30 DePietro, "Everyday Mysteries."

31 DeLillo, Americana 157.

32 DeLillo, Americana, 86.

33 DeLillo, Americana, 114.

34 DeLillo, Americana, 122–23.

35 DeLillo, Americana, 115.

36 DeLillo, Americana, 204.

37 DeLillo, Americana, 345.

38 DeLillo, Americana, 377.

39 DeLillo, Conversations, 66.

40 DeLillo, Conversations, 66.

41 DeLillo, Conversations, 67.

42 Don DeLillo, End Zone (New York: Penguin, 1972), 19.

43 DeLillo, End Zone, 30.

44 DeLillo, End Zone, 30.

45 DeLillo, Conversations, 5.

46 DeLillo, Conversations, 5.

47 DeLillo, Conversations, 5.

48 DeLillo, Conversations, 6.

49 DeLillo, Conversations, 31.

50 DeLillo, Conversations, 33.

51 DeLillo, Conversations, 34.

52 DeLillo, Conversations, 46

53 DeLillo, Conversations, 47.

54 DeLillo, End Zone 191–92.

55 Don DeLillo, Great Jones Street (New York: Penguin, 1973), 2.

56 DeLillo, Great Jones Street, 2.

57 DeLillo, Great Jones Street, 5.

58 DeLillo, Great Jones Street, 19.

59 DeLillo, Great Jones Street, 128.

60 DeLillo, Great Jones Street, 265.

61 Don DeLillo, Zero K (New York: Scribner, 2016), 3.

62 Alexandra Alter, "What Don DeLillo's Books Tell Him," The Wall Street Journal, January 30, 2010, https://tinyurl.com/y6ev3lrj.

63 DeLillo, Zero K, 14.

64 DeLillo, Zero K, 112.

65 DeLillo, Zero K, 115.

66 DeLillo, White Noise, 168.

67 Alter, "What Don DeLillo's Books Tell Him."

Chapter 4

1 Jules Siegel, "Who is Thomas Pynchon . . . and Why Did He Take Off with My Wife?" Playboy, March 1977, 122.

2 Natália Portinari, "The Fake Hermit," Piauí, May 2017, https://tinyurl.com/y457eysu.

3 Siegal, "Who is Thomas Pynchon," 122.

4 Thomas Pynchon, V. (New York: Bantam, 1964), 10–11.

5 Pynchon, V., 206.

6 Pynchon, V., 61.

7 Pynchon, V., 61.

8 Pynchon, V., 61.

9 Pynchon, V., 105.

10 Pynchon, V., 105.

11 Pynchon, V., 105.

12 Pynchon, V., 108.

13 Pynchon, V., 109.

14 Pynchon, V., 108.

15 Pynchon, V., 108.

16 Pynchon, V., 108.

17 Pynchon, V., 110.

18 Pynchon, V., 110.

19 Pynchon, V., 125.

20 Pynchon, V., 183.

21 Pynchon, V., 309.

22 Pynchon, V., 210.

23 Mel Gussow, "Pynchon's Letters Nudge His Mask," The New York Times, March 4, 1998, E8.

24 Thomas Pynchon, Slow Learner (New York: Little, Brown, 1984), 81.

25 Pynchon, Slow Learner, 82.

26 Pynchon, Slow Learner, 82.

27 Pynchon, Slow Learner, 83.

28 Pynchon, Slow Learner, 83–84.

29 Pynchon, Slow Learner, 98.

30 Pynchon, Slow Learner, 98.

31 Pynchon, Slow Learner, 12.

32 Pynchon, Slow Learner, 13.

33 Pynchon, Slow Learner, 14.

34 Pat Hackett and Andy Warhol, POPism: The Warhol '60s (New York: Harcourt Brace Jovanovich, 1980), 50.

35 Marshall McLuhan, "Casting My Perils Before Swans" in McLuhan: Hot & Cool, ed. Gerald Emanuel Stearn (New York: Dial, 1967), xi.

36 Teilhard de Chardin, The Future of Man (New York: Doubleday, 1994), 168.

37 Marshall McLuhan, Letters of Marshall McLuhan, ed. Matie Molinaro, Corinne McLuhan, and William Toye (New York: Oxford University Press, 1987), 180.

38 McLuhan, Letters, 369.

39 Tom Wolfe, Hooking Up (New York: Farrar, Straus & Giroux, 2000), 73.

40 Marshall McLuhan, The Medium is the Massage (New York: Bantam, 1967), 26.

41 McLuhan, Medium, 63.

42 McLuhan, Medium, 125.

43 McLuhan, Medium, 8.

44 Marshall McLuhan, interview with Gerald Emanuel Stearn in McLuhan: Hot & Cool (New York: Dial, 1967), 261.

45 McLuhan, interview with Stearn, 399.

46 Walter J. Ong, The Presence of the Word (Binghamton: Global Publications, 2000), 4.

47 Ong, Presence, 321.

48 Ong, Presence, 16.

49 Walter J. Ong, Orality and Literacy: The Technologizing of the Word (New York: Routledge, 1982), 151.

50 McLuhan, The Medium Is the Massage, 108–9.

51 McLuhan, Medium, 111.

52 John Richardson, "Eulogy for Andy Warhol" in The Religious Art of Andy Warhol, by Jane D. Dillenberger (New York: Continuum, 2001), 13.

53 Richardson, "Eulogy," 13.

54 Thomas Pynchon, The Crying of Lot 49 (New York: Harper Perennial, 2006), 34.

55 Pynchon, The Crying of Lot 49, 34.

56 Pynchon, The Crying of Lot 49, 14.

57 Pynchon, The Crying of Lot 49, 1.

58 Pynchon, The Crying of Lot 49, 4.

59 Pynchon, The Crying of Lot 49, 10.

60 Pynchon, The Crying of Lot 49, 24.

61 Pynchon, The Crying of Lot 49, 14.

62 Pynchon, The Crying of Lot 49, 15.

63 Pynchon, The Crying of Lot 49, 15.

64 Pynchon, The Crying of Lot 49, 150.

65 Pynchon, The Crying of Lot 49, 150–51.

66 Pynchon, The Crying of Lot 49, 61.

67 Thomas Pynchon, Gravity's Rainbow (New York: Penguin Classics, 2006), 4.

68 Pynchon, Gravity's Rainbow, 5.

69 Thomas Pynchon, Mason & Dixon (New York: Picador, 1997), 511.

70 Carl Ostrowski, "Conspiratorial Jesuits in the Postmodern Novel" in UnderWords: Perspectives on Don DeLillo's Underworld (Newark: University of Delaware Press, 2002), 96.

71 Thomas Pynchon, "Nearer, My Couch, to Thee," The New York Times, June 6, 1993, 3.

72 Pynchon, "Nearer, My Couch, to Thee," 3.

73 Pynchon, "Nearer, My Couch, to Thee," 3.

74 Pynchon, "Nearer, My Couch, to Thee," 57.

75 Pynchon, "Nearer, My Couch, to Thee," 57.

76 Pynchon, "Nearer, My Couch, to Thee," 57.

77 Pynchon, The Crying of Lot 49, 152.

Chapter 5

1 Hilton Als, "Ghosts in the House," The New Yorker, October 27, 2003, https://tinyurl.com/y5xnp72r.

2 Terry Gross, "Toni Morrison Looks Back on Her Personal Life," Fresh Air, NPR, August 24, 2015.

3 Gross, "Toni Morrison."

4 Gross, "Toni Morrison."

5 Antonio Monda, Do You Believe? (New York: Vintage, 2007), 117.

6 Monda, Do You Believe?, 117.

7 Monda, Do You Believe?, 118.

8 Monda, Do You Believe?, 121.

9 Monda, Do You Believe?, 121.

10 Monda, Do You Believe?, 121–22.

11 Monda, Do You Believe?, 119.

12 Gross, "Toni Morrison."

13 Toni Morrison, Conversations with Toni Morrison, ed. Danielle Taylor-Guthrie (Jackson: University Press of Mississippi, 1994), 4.

14 Morrison, Conversations, 61.

15 Morrison, Conversations, 115.

16 Morrison, Conversations, 116.

17 Morrison, Conversations, 117.

18 Morrison, Conversations, 45.

19 Morrison, Conversations, 78.

20 Morrison, Conversations, 97.

21 Morrison, Conversations, 152–53.

22 Morrison, Conversations, 152.

23 Morrison, Conversations, 136.

24 Toni Morrison, Toni Morrison: Conversations, ed. Carolyn C. Denard (Jackson: University Press of Mississippi, 2008), 59.

25 Morrison, Toni Morrison: Conversations, 59.

26 Toni Morrison, The Bluest Eye (New York: Penguin, 1970), 6.

27 Morrison, Bluest Eye, 9.

28 Morrison, Bluest Eye, 9.

29 Morrison, Bluest Eye, 10.

30 Morrison, Bluest Eye, 15.

31 Morrison, Bluest Eye, 15.

32 Morrison, Bluest Eye, 15.

33 Morrison, Bluest Eye, 10.

34 Morrison, Bluest Eye, 10.

35 Morrison, Bluest Eye, 12.

36 Morrison, Bluest Eye, 16.

37 Morrison, Bluest Eye, 39.

38 Morrison, Bluest Eye, 42.

39 Morrison, Bluest Eye, 126–27.

40 Morrison, Bluest Eye, 106.

41 Morrison, Bluest Eye, 20.

42 Morrison, Bluest Eye, 22.

43 Morrison, Bluest Eye, 32.

44 Morrison, Bluest Eye, 190.

45 Morrison, Bluest Eye, 190.

46 Morrison, Bluest Eye, 190.

47 Morrison, Bluest Eye, 205.

48 Morrison, Bluest Eye, 205.

49 Morrison, Bluest Eye, 187.

50 Morrison, Bluest Eye, 187.

51 Morrison, Conversations, 8.

52 Toni Morrison, Beloved (New York: Penguin, 1988), 3.

53 Morrison, Beloved, 5.

54 Morrison, Beloved, 4.

55 Morrison, Beloved, 8.

56 Morrison, Beloved, 10.

57 Morrison, Beloved, 11.

58 Morrison, Beloved, 15.

59 Morrison, Beloved, 13.

60 Morrison, Beloved, 29.

61 Morrison, Beloved, 35.

62 Morrison, Beloved, 37.

63 Morrison, Beloved, 18.

64 Morrison, Beloved, 47.

65 Morrison, Beloved, 49.

66 Morrison, Beloved, 50.

67 Morrison, Beloved, 50.

68 Morrison, Beloved, 51.

69 Morrison, Beloved, 51.

70 Morrison, Beloved, 52.

71 Morrison, Conversations, 40.

72 Morrison, Conversations, 17.

73 Morrison, Beloved, 15.

74 Morrison, Beloved, 57.

75 Morrison, Beloved, 76.

76 Morrison, Beloved, 87.

77 Morrison, Beloved, 88.

78 Morrison, Beloved, 133.

79 Morrison, Beloved, 174.

80 Morrison, Beloved, 203.

81 Morrison, Beloved, 213.

82 Morrison, Beloved, 239.

83 Morrison, Beloved, 240.

84 Morrison, Beloved, 241.

85 Morrison, Beloved, 241.

86 Morrison, Beloved, 250.

87 Morrison, Beloved, 255.

88 Morrison, Beloved, 261.

89 Morrison, Beloved, 261.

90 Morrison, Beloved, 274.

91 Morrison, Beloved, 118–19.

92 Toni Morrison, "Unspeakable Things Unspoken: The Afro-American Presence in American Literature," Michigan Quarterly Review, Winter 1989, 2.

93 Morrison, "Unspeakable Things," 8.

94 Morrison, "Unspeakable Things," 8–9.

95 Morrison, "Unspeakable Things," 19.

96 Morrison, "Unspeakable Things," 28.

97 Morrison, "Unspeakable Things," 28.

98 Toni Morrison, Paradise (New York: Knopf, 1997), 3.

99 Morrison, Paradise, 4.

100 Morrison, Paradise, 227.

101 Morrison, Paradise, 4.

102 Morrison, Paradise, 11.

103 Morrison, Paradise, 4.

104 Morrison, Paradise, 224–25.

105 Morrison, Paradise, 145.

106 Morrison, Paradise, 145–46.

107 Morrison, Paradise, 146.

108 Morrison, Paradise, 146.

109 Morrison, Paradise, 146.

110 Morrison, Paradise, 147.

111 Neanda Salvaterra, "The Pope in America: Voices," The Wall Street Journal, September 21, 2015, https://tinyurl.com/y6akzp73.

112 Dan White, "Toni Morrison and Angela Davis on Friendship and Creativity," UC Santa Cruz Review, October 29, 2014, https://tinyurl.com/yynbx65b.

Chapter 6

1   Richard B. Woodward, "Cormac McCarthy's Venomous Fiction," The New York Times, April 19, 1992, https://tinyurl.com/6xtou29.

2   Woodward, "Cormac McCarthy."

3   David Kushner, "Cormac McCarthy's Apocalypse," Rolling Stone, December 27, 2007.

4   Woodward, "Cormac McCarthy."

5   Wesley G. Morgan, "McCarthy's High School Years," The Cormac McCarthy Journal 3, no. 1 (2003).

6   Mike Gibson, "He Felt at Home Here," Metro Pulse, March 1, 2001.

7   John Jurgensen, "Hollywood's Favorite Cowboy," The Wall Street Journal, November 13 2009, https://tinyurl.com/yyvwcj9h.

8   Jurgensen, "Hollywood's Favorite Cowboy."

9   Bryan Giemza, Irish Catholic Writers and the Invention of the American South (Baton Rouge: LSU Press, 2013), 220.

10 "Book Reviews," The Virginia Quarterly Review 41, no. 3 (Summer 1965): lxxx.

11 Orville Prescott, "Still Another Disciple of William Faulkner," The New York Times, May 12, 1965, https://tinyurl.com/y2s3vun4.

12 Cormac McCarthy, The Orchard Keeper (New York: Random House, 1965), 74.

13 Ibid. 246.

14 Cormac McCarthy, Outer Dark (New York: Random House, 1968), 3.

15 McCarthy, Outer Dark, 6.

16 McCarthy, Outer Dark, 10.

17 McCarthy, Outer Dark, 15.

18 McCarthy, Outer Dark, 17.

19 McCarthy, Outer Dark, 20.

20 McCarthy, Outer Dark, 31.

21 McCarthy, Outer Dark, 32.

22 McCarthy, Outer Dark, 57.

23 Woodward, "Cormac McCarthy."

24 McCarthy, Outer Dark 154.

25 McCarthy, Outer Dark, 229.

26 McCarthy, Outer Dark, 234.

27 McCarthy, Outer Dark, 235.

28 McCarthy, Outer Dark, 235.

29 McCarthy, Outer Dark, 236.

30 McCarthy, Outer Dark, 236.

31 McCarthy, Outer Dark, 237.

32 Cormac McCarthy, Suttree (New York: Random House, 1979), 14.

33 McCarthy, Suttree, 21.

34 McCarthy, Suttree, 21.

35 McCarthy, Suttree, 66.

36 McCarthy, Suttree, 191.

37 McCarthy, Suttree, 122.

38 McCarthy, Suttree, 251.

39 McCarthy, Suttree, 253.

40 McCarthy, Suttree, 253.

41 McCarthy, Suttree, 253.

42 McCarthy, Suttree, 253.

43 McCarthy, Suttree, 253.

44 McCarthy, Suttree, 254.

45 McCarthy, Suttree, 254.

46 McCarthy, Suttree, 254.

47 McCarthy, Suttree, 254.

48 McCarthy, Suttree, 255.

49 McCarthy, Suttree, 414.

50 McCarthy, Suttree, 414.

51 McCarthy, Suttree, 460.

52 McCarthy, Suttree, 460.

53 McCarthy, Suttree, 460.

54 Cormac McCarthy, Blood Meridian (New York: Random House, 1985), 3.

55 McCarthy, Blood Meridian, 3.

56 McCarthy, Blood Meridian, 15.

57 McCarthy, Blood Meridian, 26.

58 McCarthy, Blood Meridian, 26–27.

59 McCarthy, Blood Meridian, 60.

60 McCarthy, Blood Meridian, 60.

61 McCarthy, Blood Meridian, 152.

62 McCarthy, Blood Meridian, 189.

63 McCarthy, Blood Meridian, 190.

64 McCarthy, Blood Meridian, 190.

65 McCarthy, Blood Meridian, 190–91.

66 McCarthy, Blood Meridian, 250.

67 McCarthy, Blood Meridian, 250.

68 McCarthy, Blood Meridian, 250.

69 McCarthy, Blood Meridian, 289–90.

70 Cormac McCarthy, The Road (New York: Knopf, 2006), 3.

71 McCarthy, The Road, 9.

72 McCarthy, The Road, 63.

73 McCarthy, The Road, 109.

74 McCarthy, The Road, 241.

75 Jurgensen, "Hollywood's Favorite Cowboy."

76 Cormac McCarthy, "The Kekulé Problem," Nautilus, April 20, 2017.

Chapter 7

1 "Our Story," Birchbark Books, https://tinyurl.com/y3crek94.

2 "Our Story."

3 Louise Erdrich, Conversations with Louise Erdrich & Michael Dorris, ed. Allan Chavkin and Nancy Feyl Chavkin (Jackson: University Press of Mississippi, 1994), 67–68.

4 Lisa Halliday, "Louise Erdrich, The Art of Fiction," The Paris Review, Winter 2010, https://tinyurl.com/y35jq8xs.

5 Bill Moyers, "Interview with Louise Erdrich," Bill Moyers Journal, April 9, 2010, https://tinyurl.com/y2jxl285.

6 Moyers, "Interview."

7 Erdrich, Conversations, 99.

8 Erdrich, Conversations, 230–31.

9 Moyers, "Interview."

10 Katie Beacon, "An Emissary of the Between-World," The Atlantic, January 17, 2001, https://tinyurl.com/y6x4urh5.

11 Erdrich, Conversations, 82.

12 Erdrich, Conversations, 175.

13 Louise Erdrich, Love Medicine, Newly Revised Edition (New York: Harper Perennial, 1993), 43.

14 Erdrich, Love Medicine, 43.

15 Erdrich, Love Medicine, 45.

16 Erdrich, Love Medicine, 45.

17 Erdrich, Love Medicine, 45.

18 Erdrich, Love Medicine, 45.

19 Erdrich, Love Medicine, 45.

20 Erdrich, Love Medicine, 46.

21 Erdrich, Love Medicine, 46.

22 Erdrich, Love Medicine, 46.

23 Erdrich, Love Medicine, 47.

24 Erdrich, Love Medicine, 49.

25 Erdrich, Love Medicine, 57.

26 Moyers, "Interview."

27 Louise Erdrich, The Last Report on the Miracles at Little No Horse (New York: Harper Perennial, 2001), 1.

28 Erdrich, The Last Report, 5.

29 Erdrich, The Last Report, 8.

30 Erdrich, The Last Report, 14.

31 Erdrich, The Last Report, 14.

32 Erdrich, The Last Report, 15.

33 Erdrich, The Last Report, 15–16.

34 Erdrich, The Last Report, 35.

35 Erdrich, The Last Report, 65.

36 Erdrich, The Last Report, 67.

37 Erdrich, The Last Report, 69.

38 Erdrich, The Last Report, 79.

39 Erdrich, The Last Report, 109.

40 Erdrich, The Last Report, 182.

41 Erdrich, Conversations, 45.

42 Erdrich, The Last Report, 206.

43 Erdrich, The Last Report, 207.

44 Erdrich, The Last Report, 211.

45 Erdrich, The Last Report, 221.

46 Erdrich, The Last Report, 221.

47 Louise Erdrich, The Round House (New York: HarperCollins, 2012), 74–75.

48 Erdrich, The Round House, 97.

49 Erdrich, The Round House, 315.

50 Erdrich, The Round House, 123.

51 Erdrich, The Round House, 247.

52 Erdrich, The Round House, 314.

53 Louise Erdrich, LaRose (New York: HarperCollins, 2016), 3.

54 Erdrich, LaRose, 73.

55 Erdrich, LaRose, 73.

56 Erdrich, LaRose, 8.

57 Erdrich, LaRose, 8.

58 Erdrich, LaRose, 11.

59 Erdrich, LaRose, 35.

60 Erdrich, LaRose, 35.

61 Erdrich, LaRose, 36.

62 Erdrich, LaRose, 37.

63 Erdrich, LaRose, 58.

64 Erdrich, LaRose, 245.

65 Erdrich, LaRose, 279–80.

66 Erdrich, LaRose, 280.

67 Louise Erdrich, Future Home of the Living God (New York: HarperCollins, 2017), 3.

68 Erdrich, Future Home, 3.

69 Erdrich, Future Home, 6.

70 Erdrich, Future Home, 6.

71 Erdrich, Future Home, 70.

72 Erdrich, Future Home, 70.

73 Erdrich, Future Home, 71.

74 Erdrich, Future Home, 13.

75 Rumaan Alam, "Louise Erdrich, Great American Novelist, Is Just Getting Started," Buzzfeed, November 14, 2017, https://tinyurl.com/yxeggb9n.

76 Erdrich, Future Home, 13.

77 Erdrich, Future Home, 13.

78 Erdrich, Future Home, 22.

79 Erdrich, Future Home, 22.

80 Erdrich, Future Home, 23.

81 Erdrich, Future Home, 23.

82 Erdrich, Future Home, 63.

83 Erdrich, Future Home, 64.

84 Erdrich, Future Home, 64.

85 Erdrich, Future Home, 64.

86 Erdrich, Future Home, 65.

87 Erdrich, Future Home, 66.

88 Erdrich, Future Home, 66.

89 Erdrich, Future Home, 264.

90 Erdrich, Conversations, 100.

91 Erdrich, Conversations, 155.

92 Erdrich, Conversations, 228.

93 Halliday, "Louise Erdrich."

94 Beacon, "An Emissary."

95 Moyers, "Interview."

96 Moyers, "Interview."

97 Erdrich, Conversations 155.

Chapter 8

1 Alice McDermott, That Night (New York: FSG, 1987), 4.

2 McDermott, That Night, 4.

3 McDermott, That Night, 57.

4 McDermott, That Night, 5.

5 McDermott, That Night, 18.

6 McDermott, That Night, 18.

7 McDermott, That Night, 24.

8 McDermott, That Night, 24.

9 Alice McDermott, "Confessions of a Reluctant Catholic" Commonweal, February 11, 2000, 12.

10 Paul Contino, "A Conversation with Alice McDermott," Image 52, https://tinyurl.com/y5uluze3.

11 Contino, "A Conversation."

12 Contino, "A Conversation."

13 Contino, "A Conversation."

14 Contino, "A Conversation."

15 Contino, "A Conversation."

16 Contino, "A Conversation."

17 Contino, "A Conversation."

18 Contino, "A Conversation."

19 McDermott, "Confessions," 13.

20 Contino, "A Conversation."

21 Contino, "A Conversation."

22 McDermott, "Confessions," 14.

23 McDermott, "Confessions," 15.

24 McDermott, "Confessions," 15.

25 McDermott, "Confessions," 15.

26 McDermott, "Confessions," 15.

27 Contino, "A Conversation."

28 Contino, "A Conversation."

29 Contino, "A Conversation."

30 Alice McDermott, Charming Billy (New York: FSG, 1998), 4.

31 McDermott, Charming, 12.

32 McDermott, Charming, 17.

33 McDermott, Charming, 133.

34 McDermott, Charming, 132.

35 McDermott, Charming, 133.

36 McDermott, Charming, 20.

37 McDermott, Charming, 70.

38 McDermott, Charming, 71.

39 McDermott, Charming, 110.

40 McDermott, Charming, 111

41 McDermott, Charming, 151.

42 McDermott, Charming, 154.

43 McDermott, Charming, 154.

44 McDermott, Charming, 14.

45 McDermott, Charming, 14.

46 McDermott, Charming, 161–62.

47 Alice McDermott, Someone (New York: FSG, 2013), 8.

48 McDermott, Someone, 8.

49 McDermott, Someone, 10.

50 McDermott, Someone, 10.

51 McDermott, Someone, 10.

52 McDermott, Someone, 17.

53 McDermott, Someone, 29.

54 McDermott, Someone, 88.

55 McDermott, Someone, 99.

56 McDermott, Someone, 112.

57 McDermott, Someone, 114.

58 McDermott, Someone, 170.

59 McDermott, Someone, 171.

60 McDermott, Someone, 189.

61 McDermott, Someone, 192.

62 McDermott, Someone, 226.

63 McDermott, Someone, 227.

64 Alice McDermott, The Ninth Hour (New York: FSG, 2017), 13.

65 McDermott, The Ninth Hour, 3.

66 McDermott, The Ninth Hour, 7.

67 McDermott, The Ninth Hour, 13.

68 McDermott, The Ninth Hour, 13.

69 McDermott, The Ninth Hour, 30.

70 McDermott, The Ninth Hour, 26.

71 McDermott, The Ninth Hour, 39.

72 McDermott, The Ninth Hour, 42.

73 McDermott, The Ninth Hour, 43.

74 McDermott, The Ninth Hour, 43.

75 McDermott, The Ninth Hour, 50.

76 McDermott, The Ninth Hour, 52.

77 McDermott, The Ninth Hour, 52.

78 McDermott, The Ninth Hour, 66.

79 McDermott, The Ninth Hour, 85.

80 McDermott, The Ninth Hour, 88.

81 McDermott, The Ninth Hour, 91.

82 McDermott, The Ninth Hour, 183.

83 Paul Elie, "The Ignatian Imagination: A Veteran's Perspective," Georgetown University Berkley Center, November 13, 2018, https://tinyurl.com/yydrjood.

84 "Phil Klay: Catholic Poet & Patriot," America Films, November 11, 2018, https://tinyurl.com/y3vgu62y.

85 Nick Ripatrazone, "A Conversation with Phil Klay," Image Journal, Winter 2015, 68.

86 Phil Klay, Redeployment (New York: Penguin, 2014), 32.

87 Klay, Redeployment, 45–46.

88 Klay, Redeployment, 46.

89 Klay, Redeployment, 46.

90 Klay, Redeployment, 129.

91 Klay, Redeployment, 129.

92 Klay, Redeployment, 131.

93 Klay, Redeployment, 132.

94 Klay, Redeployment, 132.

95 Klay, Redeployment, 132.

96 Klay, Redeployment, 134.

97 Klay, Redeployment, 137.

98 Klay, Redeployment, 138.

99 Klay, Redeployment, 139.

100 Klay, Redeployment, 139.

101 Klay, Redeployment, 142.

102 Klay, Redeployment, 145.

103 Klay, Redeployment, 145.

104 Klay, Redeployment, 147.

105 Klay, Redeployment, 150.

106 Klay, Redeployment, 150.

107 Klay, Redeployment, 151.

108 Klay, Redeployment, 152.

109 Klay, Redeployment, 154.

110 Klay, Redeployment, 156.

111 Klay, Redeployment, 156.

112 Klay, Redeployment, 167.

113 Klay, Redeployment, 167.

114 Klay, Redeployment, 167.

115 Ripatrazone, "A Conversation," 65.

116 Ripatrazone, "A Conversation," 66.

117 Ripatrazone, "A Conversation," 68.

118 Ripatrazone, "A Conversation," 69.

119 Ripatrazone, "A Conversation."

120 Alice McDermott, "Redeemed from Death? The Faith of a Catholic Novelist," Commonweal, May 3, 2013, https://tinyurl.com/yygoa9fe.

INDEX